THE LOWER BATTLEFIELD *of* ANTIETAM

THE LOWER BATTLEFIELD *of* ANTIETAM

The Forgotten Front of America's Bloodiest Day

Robert M. Dunkerly

The History Press

Published by The History Press
An imprint of Arcadia Publishing
Charleston, SC
www.historypress.com

Front cover: "Fighting on the Ridges," by Dale Gallon, https://www.gallon.com.

First published 2025

Manufactured in the United States

ISBN 9781467159289

Library of Congress Control Number: 2025934494

Dedicated to Corporal Samuel Dunkerly, Company F, Forty-Eighth Pennsylvania

and

Dr. Peter S. Carmichael, Robert C. Fluhrer Professor of Civil War Studies and Director of the Civil War Institute at Gettysburg College

One fought here; the other preserved its legacy.

CONTENTS

PROLOGUE

Antietam is one of my favorite battlefields. The terrain, the maneuvering, the convergence of political and military events in the campaign and the commemoration of those events are all unique and fascinating. I recall visiting for the first time in the 1980s; it was incredible to see the places I had read about and tried to envision. Over the years, I visited regularly and studied it intently. I have a personal connection to the battle and to this story in particular. An ancestor, Corporal Samuel Dunkerly, served in the Forty-Eighth Pennsylvania. Seeing that unit's monument was, and remains, a highlight for me.

I was also struck by how parts of the battlefield seemed well-preserved and interpreted, but the lower area where the Forty-Eighth Pennsylvania and the Ninth Corps fought was not. I could not grasp or articulate why this was or why it bothered me. In time, I came to understand the battlefield's preservation history and studied this part of the battle and the battlefield more intensely.

I recall stopping on the driving tour route, a narrow lane of park property, bounded on both sides by a fence and private land, and looking in both directions. I could see the land where the fighting occurred, but I could not access it. I noticed monuments out in the field, several hundred yards away. *Why were they there?* I wondered. *Could I ever see them?* I yearned to walk that land. Eventually, as the park preserved more property, I could. The best way to appreciate a battlefield is by walking the land; nothing can equal the soldiers' perspective. In addition, those monuments and their dedications were important historic events and tie into the history of the park and the battle's memory.

Thankfully, through the diligent work of park staff and preservationists, more of this area is now preserved, accessible and interpreted with well-planned trails, markers and brochures. In fact, Antietam's efforts to preserve land and make the battlefield accessible to the public are, in my opinion, cutting edge. This is a fascinating, important and underappreciated part of the battle.

ACKNOWLEDGEMENTS

Thank you to John Rodrigue, acquisitions editor at The History Press, for his support; Roxanne Bowman for extraordinary hospitality; John Coski and Robert Hancock with the American Civil War Museum; Kevin Pawlak with Bristoe Station Battlefield; librarian Kathy Shoemaker; Jenny Palter, Washington County (MD) Library; author Michael Hardy; Keith Snyder, Brian Baracz, Stephanie Gray and Mark Cheney with Antietam National Battlefield; Ranger John Hoptak of Gettysburg National Military Park; reviewer Kate Egner-Gruber; Elena Peters with the Connecticut Historical Society, and Scott Hartwig for permission to use his maps. A group of friends joined me in hiking the route of A.P. Hill's division to the battlefield, something I've always wanted to do. Crossing the Potomac at Pack Horse Ford was very special that day. Thanks to Rich Condon, Drew Gruber, Jim Broomall, Richard Lewis and Kevin Pawlak for a great day; the insights we gained were invaluable. Thanks to G.G. and Lee Steelman for their hospitality while I was finishing the edits. As always, Sarah Nance supports me in everything I do, and thank you Albert and Frank for your good company.

INTRODUCTION

Of all the days on all the fields where American soldiers have fought, the most terrible by almost any measure was September 17, 1862. The battle waged on that date, close by Antietam Creek at Sharpsburg in western Maryland, took a human toll never exceeded on any other single day in the nation's history. So intense and sustained was the violence, a man recalled, that for a moment in his mind's eye the very landscape around him turned red.

—Stephen W. Sears, Landscape Turned Red

Visit Antietam National Battlefield in Maryland and take the park's driving tour, the recommended way to get the most out of a visit. You will initially pass through vast areas of park property, where you can park, walk numerous trails and inspect monuments and markers. Until recently, this was not the case in the southern portion of the park. This part of the Antietam battlefield has been largely neglected: by contemporary historians, by Civil War photographers like Alexander Gardner and even by the creators of the battlefield park itself. It did not involve nearly the numbers of troops or commanders that the northern and central portions of the battlefield did. Nor were some of the more famous personalities present here: Longstreet, Jackson, Hooker and Sumner all were involved in or supervised the fighting to the north. The most famous units in both armies—the Iron Brigade, the Texas Brigade, the Irish Brigade, the Stonewall Brigade—all fought in the upper part of the battle.

As a major battle of the Civil War, Antietam is one of the most studied, discussed and debated engagements of the conflict. Attention is usually focused on the northern areas of the battlefield, where the fighting began and the most casualties occurred. The bulk of the day's combat happened there, where the largest portion of the armies fought. The upper area also has famous landmarks like the West Woods, the North Woods, the Cornfield, the Sunken Road and Dunker Church. The southern area of the battlefield is the most neglected, both historically and in modern studies.

This part of the field is the only area where the Confederates used Antietam Creek as a barrier and thus the only part where Union troops had to force their way across. The lower field may as well have been a different battle entirely. The Ninth Corps fought alone, without any direct support, the only Union corps to fight unassisted at Antietam. My intention is not to criticize McClellan's management of the battle. Rather, this book seeks to study in detail the final phase of the battle and explore lingering issues and unknowns for which we may never have answers.

Our general understanding is also oversimplified by focusing on the Rohrbach (Burnside's) Bridge and A.P. Hill's counterattack. The Union struggle to capture the Rohrbach Bridge and the accompanying inept leadership are certainly a crucial part of the story. Hill's arrival in the nick of time and at the right place was a made-for-Hollywood moment. Yet in between were important actions that have been largely neglected, such as the advance of General Isaac Rodman's and General Orlando Willcox's divisions—late-day drives that nearly succeeded.

The disjointed Union advance after capturing the bridge was crucial to how events unfolded that afternoon. How and why it occurred and how it affected the rest of the engagement are crucial to the engagement's outcome. Much of this area could not be accessed or studied in detail until its acquisition by the park in 2003.

The Union troops that fought on the southern portion of the battlefield were newcomers to the Army of the Potomac: the Ninth Corps. They had joined the army in time for the Battle of Second Manassas in late August and thus did not have a long association with it as some of the other corps did. By the afternoon of September 17, the lower part of the battlefield, the Ninth Corps' sector, had become the only active part of the field and the only place where the battle's outcome could be determined.

The overshadowing of the southern portion of the battlefield began in the days after the fighting ended. In the battle's aftermath, photographer

Alexander Gardner spent most of his time taking his dramatic photos in the now more famous northern areas, and by the time he reached the southern end of the field, most of the dead had been removed. While he took many images of Burnside's Bridge, there were no other major landmarks or natural features that captured the public's imagination as did those sites to the north. Gardner took few images of the areas of the final attacks that afternoon.[1]

While the upper area has been well-preserved and includes the most significant areas of fighting, until the mid-2000s, that was not the case with the lower area. Preserved land is important, for it affects what we can see and access and therefore what we can more easily study. In this way, a historic site, and how it is preserved and interpreted, serves as a lens through which we understand the past and impacts our perceptions. What is preserved—or not—also affects our ability to understand and study the past. Currently, the park's driving tour has seven stops in the upper and middle parts of the battlefield, with only two in the lower part. Visitors pass through areas of heavy combat and complex maneuver with little idea of what happened there. An entire part of the battle and its concluding actions have been little studied as a result.

The War Department created Antietam National Battlefield in 1890, and the National Park Service acquired it in 1933. South of the Boonsboro Pike, the park acquired only a thin strip of land, following property lines, for a tour route. Along this line, veterans placed monuments and the War Department installed metal plaques. The land where the actual fighting took place was not preserved but could be viewed from the tour road. This approach, which soon came to be called the Antietam Plan, would be replicated in other battlefield parks to avoid costly and controversial land acquisition but allow visitors to view the terrain.

The War Department placed metal plaques, as it did at other military parks, to note the position and actions of various units. Through the 1890s and early 1900s, Union veterans placed monuments to their regiments and batteries: often along the tour road, more rarely on private land where they actually fought. The area between the Boonsboro Pike and the sharp bend in Antietam Creek downstream from the Burnside Bridge conveniently encloses the lower area of the battlefield. A narrow access path led to the Ninth New York (Hawkins' Zouaves) monument, but otherwise nearly the entire area was inaccessible and unpreserved. The National Park Service appreciated the significance of this area, and in the early 2000s, the park was able to acquire the land south of the Ninth New York monument, saving a large chunk of battlefield land. In 2003, the area between the tour road and the bridge was acquired, preserving even more critical areas of fighting at the Otto and Sherrick farm sites.

The Ninth Corps that fought here had a unique relationship with the Army of the Potomac during the Civil War. Mirroring their involvement with the army was that of their best-known commander, Ambrose Burnside. The corps itself only existed for a month prior to the Maryland Campaign. It was also a newcomer to the army in 1862, part of it having joined in time to fight at Second Manassas. These Ninth Corps troops had a variety of origins and were brought together to form a corps. Some had begun the war in western Virginia, others on the North Carolina coast. They then transferred to service in Virginia. At Newport News in July 1862, three divisions combined to establish the Ninth Corps. The entire corps of four divisions then joined in the pursuit of the Confederate army across Maryland just a week before the battle at Antietam.[2]

The Kanawha Division also joined the corps before Antietam. Composed of six Ohio regiments, the division was transferred away after Antietam, their only major battle and their only one with the Army of the Potomac. Thus, the Ninth Corps and its units do not have a long or storied association with the army as did the First, Second, Fifth or Sixth Corps. Even its corps badge is different: rather than a simple shape like the others, it features a shield with a crossed cannon and anchor, reflecting the corps' participation in amphibious operations in North Carolina early in the war.

After Fredericksburg, the corps was transferred west, fighting at Vicksburg and Knoxville, and then back to Virginia for the 1864 Overland Campaign. They were the only corps to fight in the east with the Army of the Potomac, move to the western theater and then return to Virginia. Most of the other corps of the army had served together in the Peninsula and then the Seven Days' Campaigns. There, they established their reputations and created their own culture. The Ninth Corps was not part of that shared experience (nor did it participate in the army's greatest victory, Gettysburg).

There was little time for these separate commands making up the Ninth Corps to work together or form a sense of identity in September 1862, crucial for entering combat at Antietam. The corps had another challenge: many of its units were brand-new or had very limited combat experience. Some were fighting for the first time or had only fought in one major battle: Second Manassas or South Mountain. For units like the 100th Pennsylvania, Sixteenth Connecticut, Seventeenth Michigan, Thirty-Fifth

Ninth Corps flag. *Division of Military and Society, National Museum of American History, Smithsonian Institution.*

Massachusetts and Ninth New Hampshire, Antietam would be their first battle. Several others, including the Thirtieth Ohio and 103rd New York, had seen some combat but were hardly seasoned veterans. They were as green as the rookie units. Much like at the brigade and division command level, there was little chance for units or commanders to build working relationships. The Sixteenth Connecticut was not only brand-new, but it had also just arrived, marching into camp the night before the battle.[3]

On September 14, General George B. McClellan created wings for the army, with General Ambrose Burnside commanding a wing with the First and Ninth Corps. McClellan created these wings to expedite the army's movement out of Washington, D.C., and to cover the three approaches toward Frederick. General Jesse Reno rose to command the Ninth Corps but was killed at South Mountain later that day. With Reno killed, General Jacob D. Cox assumed corps command. Burnside allowed Reno's staff to accompany the general's body to Washington for the funeral, a moving gesture but one that also reduced the available staff officers for Burnside and Cox for the coming battle. Cox noted that on returning from a meeting with McClellan on the evening of September 16, Burnside was "disturbed and grieved at the course things had taken" with the breakup of his wing. It was not a good mindset for a commander who would be expected to play a major role in a coming battle.

Scholars are divided about the creation and abandonment of the wing system. Historian Scott Hartwig theorizes the move may have been politically motivated, suggesting General-in-Chief Henry Halleck urged the wing system on McClellan, who adopted it reluctantly. McClellan mistrusted his senior corps commander, Major General Edwin V. Sumner, and Burnside was a close friend until McClellan learned of Burnside writing to Lincoln and Halleck criticizing Porter, a close confidant of McClellan. Or it may have been impractical and unwieldy, as historians Kevin Pawlak and Ethan Rafuse argue. Historian Gary Gallagher notes the impact on Burnside's mindset and resulting influence on his actions and mood. After the battle of South Mountain, the First Corps moved toward Sharpsburg rapidly while the Ninth did not, separating them and making coordination difficult. The important point is that the wing system was abruptly ended, with no instructions on how to proceed without it.[4]

McClellan never made it clear why he implemented the wing system, what he expected of it or why he suddenly abandoned it on the eve of battle. Burnside now reverted to corps command—or at least commanding only one corps, as the First Corps ended up on the other side of the battlefield from the Ninth. McClellan's orders came to Burnside, and he passed them on to Cox. Burnside thought that the detachment of the First Corps was only temporary. Thus, he and Cox would have to develop a way to handle managing their corps, and in this they failed. At times Burnside interceded, and at times Cox directed the corps. If they made some sort of verbal agreement about coordinating, there is no record of it. Throughout the day, both commanders stepped in, giving orders to brigades and even regiments. This created an uncoordinated command structure that impacted the Ninth Corps' ability to maneuver and fight effectively.[5]

With Cox in nominal corps command, this created a ripple effect that reverberated through the corps. It elevated Colonel Eliakim P. Scammon to command the Kanawha Division and Colonel Hugh Ewing to command a brigade. Could Burnside have inquired of McClellan how to proceed? Could McClellan have clarified the situation and what he expected? Could Cox or Burnside have tried to decide between them how to handle the situation? Did it make Cox cautious in not wanting to act aggressively and appear to undercut Burnside? These are lingering questions that must be recognized in our analysis of Antietam.[6]

General Cox was capable but had never commanded a corps in battle. Now four division commanders reported to him, and he oversaw thirteen thousand men, a challenging task even for an experienced leader. Among the four division commanders, Samuel Sturgis, Orlando Willcox and Isaac Rodman had limited experience leading a division in battle, and Eliakim Scammon had none at all.

Despite being overlooked and not as famous, the lower portion of the Antietam battlefield witnessed drama, courage and carnage nearly equal to that of the more renowned areas like the Cornfield, the West Woods and Bloody Lane. Several units suffered losses of 50 percent or more. Most histories tend to gloss over the role of the Ninth Corps, oversimplify its slow start and neatly close with A.P. Hill's late-day counterattack.

What played out on the lower end of the battlefield was a series of sharp actions that have too long been overlooked in histories of the battle. Ironically, the battle's most famous landmark, the Burnside (Rohrbach) Bridge is here, and it was here that a soldier remarked how the landscape around him turned red. A future U.S. president served here: William McKinley. Colonel Harrison Fairchild's brigade suffered the highest percentage of casualties for any Union brigade of the entire battle.[7]

The facts are that the unsupported Ninth Corps had a difficult task in taking the bridge, made more so by the tenacity of a few hundred Georgians. Difficult terrain and an ideally defendable position account for much of the difficulty in taking the bridge. Merely looking at the disparity in manpower misses critical points. Numbers alone do not tell the story, for all the Confederate troops involved were veterans, and many of the Union regiments were untested. In addition, the poor Federal performance can also be partially attributed to the inefficient command structure of the Ninth Corps and McClellan's lack of support for them.

The Battle of Antietam began at the upper (northern) end and saw the most ferocious fighting at the Cornfield, the West Woods and nearby areas. From midmorning until midday, fighting shifted to the center at the Sunken Road. Then, in the afternoon, the fighting intensified at the lower end of the battlefield and the engagement reached its indecisive climax there. A.P. Hill's late-day counterattack was actually more limited than and not as devastating as is generally believed, but sharp fighting did ensue across the slopes and fields below Sharpsburg.

The details of the flow of combat through the Cornfield and into the West Woods, as well as the advance on the Sunken Road, are well documented in Antietam studies. Not so the combat on Otto's ridge, the forty-acre cornfield,

Sherrick's orchard and Otto's farm lane. Again, many histories speak in general terms or paint with broad brushstrokes in describing these actions, yet intense fighting ensued across the slopes and fields below Sharpsburg, and it deserves a more detailed look.

All this is not to say that the fighting in the southern area was of equal scale to that above it or that A.P. Hill's attack was insignificant. Yet our study of Antietam seems unbalanced; it is time to take another look at this area and examine these questions in greater detail.

Chapter 1

TO TAKE THE BRIDGE

In September 1862, when the Confederate army invaded Maryland following its victory at Second Manassas, Union forces were in disarray. The Lincoln administration relieved General John Pope and recalled General George B. McClellan to take command of the Army of the Potomac. Various units were pulled together in Washington, D.C., to move out after the Confederates.

Lee's army reached Frederick, Maryland, on September 7 and then turned west. Lee divided his army: part of it went to surround the Union garrison at Harpers Ferry, and other units moved to Hagerstown for the next phase, the invasion of Pennsylvania. Yet in one of the most incredible twists of fate, a copy of Lee's orders outlining his troop positions fell into Union hands. The information, found by soldiers at a Confederate campsite near Frederick, gave McClellan Lee's plans and allowed him to move to strike at the scattered Confederates.

On September 14, Union forces attacked the Confederates holding the passes at South Mountain, west of Hagerstown. By the end of the day, the three gaps were in Union hands, and the Confederates pulled back toward the town of Sharpsburg. Here, Lee, informed of Stonewall Jackson's impending capture of Harpers Ferry and seeking to salvage the campaign, made the decision to stand and fight rather than withdraw back to Virginia. The Army of the Potomac began arriving near Antietam Creek on September 15. McClellan deployed the greater part of his forces on his right, with one corps at the center and the Ninth Corps on the army's left.

General Ambrose E. Burnside. *Library of Congress.*

General Ambrose Burnside originally commanded the Ninth Corps and then was elevated to wing command over this and the First Corps. When Burnside took over his wing, General Jesse Reno was elevated to corps command. But Reno was killed at South Mountain, so corps command went to General Jacob D. Cox. On September 16, General McClellan scrapped the wing system abruptly, without providing further instructions. Following the wing's breakup, Burnside returned to corps command, sharing it with Cox, though he insisted that he still commanded a wing.[8]

The Ninth Corps also faced the most difficult terrain of any Union troops at Antietam. They had the challenge of crossing the creek, and beyond it, the ground was hilly, with a deep ravine. This landscape included several wooden fences and stone walls, some with worm fencing atop them. The terrain made maneuver and communication difficult and, perhaps most importantly, blocked lines of sight.

There were also simply not enough Union troops on this part of the field to exploit any breakthrough. The bulk of the Union army was to the north, unable to assist. The roughly thirteen thousand men of the Ninth Corps were insufficient to attack and occupy the ground assigned to them. Compared to the upper parts of the battlefield, the Ninth Corps was being asked to advance and occupy an area that two corps or more would do elsewhere.

McClellan stated that his plan was "to make the main attack upon the enemy's left—at least to create a diversion in favor of the main attack, with the hope of something more by assailing the enemy's right." That would be the Ninth Corps. His orders were not clear whether Burnside was to attack at the same time with Hooker, on the far right, or wait until the enemy was weakened by Hooker's assault. Months later, McClellan wrote,

> *My plan...was to attack the enemy's left with the corps of Hooker and Mansfield, supported by Sumner's...and as soon as matters looked favorably there, to move the corps of Burnside against the enemy's extreme right....The attack on the right was to have been supported by an attack on the left.*

Both statements are ambiguous, and the goal here is not to examine McClellan's generalship but only to note that his orders at the time were vague.[9]

The battle began on the north end on the evening of September 16 as the First Corps moved into position for the next day's assault. Fighting resumed at about five thirty on the upper end of the field the next morning, where the Union First and Twelfth Corps attacked Jackson's command. Fighting seesawed back and forth for several hours, each side steadily feeding in more troops. Next the Union Second Corps assaulted the West Woods and the Sunken Road. All the while there was action on the southern end of the field as well.

Originally, two Confederate divisions (D.R. Jones's and John G. Walker's) guarded the army's right flank behind the Rohrbach bridge. As fighting raged to the north, Lee sent Walker's division and part of Jones's to bolster the army's left. Having dispatched two brigades to the north, Jones retained those of Toombs, Drayton, Kemper and Jenkins, about 2,430 men.[10]

Relatively unknown today, David R. Jones was born in South Carolina and raised in Georgia. He attended West Point, graduating in the class of 1846, where McClellan was a classmate. The thirty-seven-year-old was nicknamed Neighbor for his friendly demeanor. He married Sarah Taylor, the daughter of former President Zachary Taylor, and was also cousin to President Jefferson Davis. His brother-in-law, Henry Kingsbury, was colonel of the Eleventh Connecticut that was lined up across Antietam Creek.

General David R. Jones. *Heyward Album, South Caroliniana Library.*

Jones had risen quickly; he had only led a division since Second Manassas. Later that fall, he became ill with a heart condition, and he died in Richmond in January. He is buried in Hollywood Cemetery. His full potential as a commander will forever be unknown. Like the rest of the Army of Northern Virginia, Jones's and A.P. Hill's divisions contained understrength brigades, weakened by losses in the Battles of the Seven Days, Second Manassas and the Maryland Campaign. In fact, from late May until now, the troops had been nearly constantly marching and fighting.[11]

Jones deployed his division with the bulk of his force along high ground near Sharpsburg, about half a mile west of the Rohrbach Bridge. Only one brigade, led by General Robert Toombs, was along the creek, overlooking the bridge. The fiery Georgia politician placed the Second and Twentieth Georgia on the high ground overlooking the bridge, and downstream to cover Snavely's Ford was the Fiftieth Georgia (borrowed from Drayton's brigade) and two companies of South Carolinians between the Second and Fiftieth Georgia.[12]

General Toombs was a fifty-one-year-old Georgia native and son of a Revolutionary War veteran. Known for his temper and strong personality, he would need every bit of tenacity at Antietam. He ordered Colonel Henry Benning of the Seventeenth Georgia to oversee the placement of troops at the bridge and along the creek on the Fifteenth. Not long after, Toombs had Benning detach two regiments to the rear to protect wagons from Union cavalry. Thus the Fifteenth and Seventeenth Georgia were sent away, reducing the frontline strength of the defenders.[13]

Benning placed the Twentieth Georgia on his left, on the high ground behind the bridge and to the north. Some used a stone quarry above the bridge for shelter. On the right he had the Second Georgia, on the high ground below the bridge and parallel to the road on the other side of the creek. The troops pulled the fence rails down from the road and built barricades with them. George McRae of the Twentieth Georgia described how they scattered along the heights above the bridge so that they were "shooting over the head of those in front…some behind trees, some behind rocks and others in some depressions in the hillside."[14]

General Robert Toombs. *Library of Congress.*

Benning estimated that the Second Georgia had only 97 men (Private Theodore Fogle writes only 89) and the Twentieth about 250. Thus roughly 350 men were on the front line guarding the creek. With the Fiftieth Georgia (about 150) farther to the right, these small units covered a mile of ground.[15]

Geroge McRea of the Twentieth Georgia recalled that they were so well hidden by rocks, trees and logs that when the attack began, "we spring from our hiding places they saw us for the first time and opened fire on us." J.W. Lokey of the same regiment noted that they "made temporary breast works."[16]

Two hundred yards behind Toombs's men, along Otto Lane, were two batteries of artillery. The ridge offered a good position for these guns: Captain Benjamin F. Eshelman's and Captain John Richardson's batteries, the Second and Fourth Companies, respectively, of the Washington Artillery of New Orleans. Each fielded four smoothbore guns. Eshleman pulled out at noon to cover Snavely's Ford to the south, and Richardson withdrew to the west around one o'clock, where his guns fired on the Union advance that began around three o'clock in the afternoon. Captain James S. Brown's Wise (Virginia) Battery of four guns was also located along Otto Lane and supported Toombs until they withdrew when the bridge fell.[17]

John and Katherine Otto, their children and two enslaved people left their home the day before the battle, seeking safety south of town. The house, built around 1833, stood along the road from Sharpsburg to the Rohrbach Bridge, across from the Sherrick Farm. The Ottos had a springhouse, a detached kitchen, a barn, a root cellar, a hog pen and other outbuildings by 1862.[18]

Their slave Hillary Watson recalled, "Early in the morning on the Monday before the battle of Antietam the Rebels came in hyar, and the hill at our place was covered with 'em. They'd walk right into the house and say, 'Have you got anything to eat?' like they was half starved. We'd hardly fix up for a couple when a lot mo' would come in." Private J.W. Lokey, with the Twentieth Georgia overlooking the bridge, noted, "We had been two days without rations. I, with a detail, was sent to the rear to get some rations for the men." They likely visited Otto's farm.[19]

The Rohrbach (Burnside) Bridge looms large in studies of the final phase of the battle. Generations of park visitors and many writers have looked at the bridge and oversimplified the task before the Ninth Corps. While it seems easy enough to charge over the bridge and seems equally absurd that a few hundred could hold off several thousand, the reality is much more complicated. Historian John Hoptak has noted that the arithmetic was horrific: 350 seasoned Confederate soldiers firing twice a minute meant 700 bullets per minute aimed at a very narrow front and a bridge opening only a few feet wide.

Perched on the high ground above the bridge on the west side, the Georgia soldiers under Toombs could command every conceivable approach from the east. Furthermore, the road approaching the bridge ran alongside the creek with a rail fence parallel to it. This would funnel any attacker into a

The Rohrbach Bridge. *Author.*

narrow lane for over five hundred yards before even reaching the bridge. All the while, they would be exposed to enemy fire from the front and flank.

John Hudson of the Thirty-Fifth Massachusetts noted the good cover that shielded the Confederates: "The rebs were posted behind trees & natural projections of the rocky, wood covered, slope, along the brow of the slope, behind little curious shelters made of rails, in form of small lunettes & provided with loopholes…and in a few cases up in the trees."[20]

Both Burnside and Cox failed to properly prepare their corps for the attack. The bridge that would occupy their attention initially and would be forever linked to this part of the battle was a limestone structure with three arches, typical of others in the region. It was twelve feet wide and 125 feet long and had wooden parapets on the top of the two sides.

It was a remarkably attractive bridge, but its narrow width made it a bottleneck, permitting only a small number to cross at a time. In fact, this would be a problem long after the bridge was taken, for it hampered the efforts of the Ninth Corps the rest of the day. Any reinforcements, withdrawing troops, wounded men, artillery or supply wagons had to cross this narrow passage on which traffic could only move one way.

There is a lot of missing information regarding the fords and the search for them, and this is a crucial part of events here. On September 16, Captain of Engineers James Duane had been sent by McClellan to find a ford for crossing the creek below the bridge that was known to local residents (Snavely's Ford). He located one ford about a mile below the bridge but did not look for any others, above or below the stone structure.[21]

Did Duane find a ford that turned out to be too shallow for Rodman's division the next day, with the banks too steep and the site within range of the South Carolina troops on the other side? Did Duane find Snavely's Ford but fail to mark it or properly inform Rodman's staff where it was? Duane left no account of his scouting.

McClellan also tasked Duane with posting Burnside's divisions so they were ready to jump off in the morning. Using three of Burnside's aides, Duane assigned the divisions their places for the evening. Why McClellan had this done in this manner, bypassing Burnside and Cox, is unclear.[22]

The night of September 16, the Union soldiers settled in, ate their rations and prepared for battle the next day as a misty, drizzly rain set in. One soldier in the Seventy-Ninth New York described it as a heavy rainstorm. The men of the new Sixteenth Connecticut loaded their muskets for the very first time that evening. One soldier's weapon accidentally went off, his first shot as a solider—thankfully, not injuring anyone.[23]

The Union troops of the Ninth Corps who bedded down on the evening of September 16 did not even know the name of creek in front of them, and few had any idea of where exactly it was. Nor did they know the precise location of the bridge itself or the roads approaching it. Some didn't even know there was a creek or bridge.[24]

The next day, orders from headquarters arrived at "about seven," according to Cox, instructing them to prepare to attack. Of course, the battle had already begun on the other side of the field. Or was this an attack order that Burnside and Cox misunderstood? Did Burnside and Cox have a clear understanding of the larger battle plan and their role in it? The two made little effort to scout the terrain or encourage their subordinates to do so. It would become painfully clear that the Union troops knew only that the creek and bridge were somewhere in front of them.[25]

After seven o'clock in the morning, the Ninth Corps advanced to its jump-off point, not knowing exactly what was in front of them. Closest to the bridge was General Samuel D. Sturgis's division. On the left, poised to seek the ford and cross below the bridge, was General Isaac P. Rodman's division. On the right, ready to do the same above the span, was General

Orlando B. Willcox's division. The Kanawha division under Colonel Eliakim P. Scammon was split, with one brigade assisting Rodman and the other supporting Sturgis. Cox sent Rodman's division with Ewing's brigade to the south to find Snavely's Ford. It was known to be in that vicinity, but no one in the division had scouted the route or its exact location, and the delay impacted the Ninth Corps' effectiveness. Cox noted that crossing the ford was an important part of the overall plan to cross the creek. Doing so would turn the Confederate army's flank, provide access to its rear and cut it off from escape.[26]

In McClellan's August 1863 report, he claimed that he ordered Burnside to attack at 8:00 a.m., but it seems those orders were to get ready, which Burnside did, moving troops into position and awaiting further instructions. Either McClellan's memory was faulty, or he was covering his mistakes. Hearing of no progress, army headquarters sent an order to attack at 9:10 a.m., which Burnside and Cox note arrived at about 10:00 a.m.[27]

The battle opened at about 5:30 a.m. with Union attacks on the Confederate left at the Cornfield, about three miles to the north. By ten o'clock, the battle there had been raging for four hours and had already produced twelve thousand casualties. McClellan wanted to take pressure off his forces in that sector and again urged Burnside to make progress. Burnside ordered General Samuel D. Sturgis to attack the bridge after receiving McClellan's 9:10 order. General Cox went forward to personally supervise.[28]

Just after nine o'clock, as fighting raged to the north, Lee pulled General John G. Walker's division of two brigades out to assist the Confederate left. His force, which had only arrived at sunrise, was guarding the high ground above Snavely's Ford. Now that task fell to Toombs' Fiftieth Georgia, who had to spread themselves to cover a wider area.[29]

The first attempt on the bridge, the most obvious point of attack for the defending Georgians, was badly managed. Colonel George Crook was to send his Ohio brigade forward to the bridge, under covering fire from Colonel Henry W. Kingsbury's Eleventh Connecticut. Crook, best known today for fighting in the Indian Wars in the West in the 1870s and '80s, had been in command for only five days. His lack of preparation was apparent when he asked the aide, "What bridge?"[30]

At about ten o'clock, the New Englanders charged along the road that led to the bridge to take up position and provide covering fire. The entire way, they were exposed in the open and confined to the road, which was bordered by the creek on their left and a rail fence on their right. Most of the men

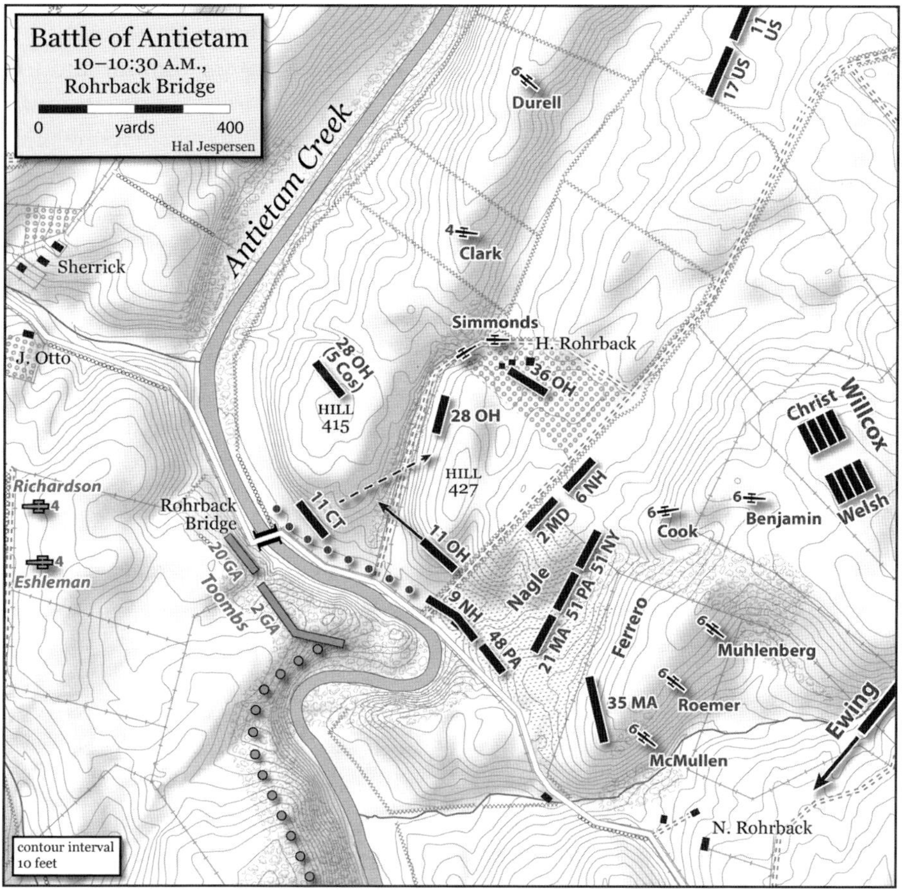

Map of troop positions at 10:00 a.m. *Hal Jespersen.*

fired all sixty rounds they had been issued, and some even took cartridges from the dead and wounded.[31]

Colonel Kingsbury led the left wing across the open ground under tremendous fire while Captain John Griswold led the right. Griswold led a small group splashing into the creek just below the bridge, but most were struck down. Griswold was hit and fell on the west bank of the creek. The New Englanders fell back in disarray. Kingsbury tried to rally his men but was shot in the foot and leg. As he was carried off the field, he was hit again, in the shoulder and in the abdomen. Kingsbury was taken to the Rohrbach farmhouse for treatment, where General Burnside came to check on him; Burnside had met him years before at West Point. Kingsbury passed away, and three months later back in Connecticut, his son was born.[32]

Crook's attack, meant to take the bridge, was a disaster. The Ohio troops charged, emerging three hundred yards north of the bridge, missing it entirely. Two companies of the Eleventh Ohio of Crook's command had been on the high ground just east of the bridge for hours, surveying the ground and the Confederate positions beyond. When Burnside and Cox ordered the assault on the bridge, either the messenger, Lieutenant Samuel Christie, or Colonel Crook misunderstood. Crook claimed to not know the location of the bridge or even the creek (despite one of his units being in position overlooking both for hours). Crook apparently thought he would follow Sturgis's division, not lead the attack, and did not even know which direction to move. It was one of many breakdowns on the federal side this day.[33]

The Eleventh Ohio endured punishing fire as they charged downhill from the woods toward the creek, only to find no bridge in sight. They had emerged well north of their target. Disoriented and taking heavy casualties, they fell back to the safety of the wooded slope from which they came. Colonel Augustus H. Coleman was hit and died a few hours later. The Eleventh Ohio lost twenty-one men this day, most of them in this morning assault. It was all over in about thirty minutes.[34]

General Cox observed the attack, noting, "Our advance upon the bridge could only be made by a narrow column, showing a front of eight men at most; but the front from which Toombs deployed behind his defences was three or four hundred yards both above and below the bridge." He also noted that the Confederate batteries had "the exact range of the little valley." Throughout the morning as the attacks unfolded against the bridge, Cox kept hoping to hear from Rodman about his progress finding a crossing. The silence must have been frustrating.[35]

General Jacob D. Cox. *Library of Congress.*

General James Nagle's brigade of Sturgis's division launched the next assault on the bridge around eleven o'clock. Nagle ordered the Second Maryland and the Sixth New Hampshire to rush the bridge, while the Ninth New Hampshire and Forty-Eighth Pennsylvania provided covering fire from wooded high ground to the east. The New Englanders fired from the ground, rolling over on their backs to reload. This next assault went forward at around eleven o'clock and fared no better. Side by side, the two regiments fixed bayonets and ran toward the narrow opening in the rail fence that ran along the road to the bridge. Colonel Simon G. Griffin lead the way under heavy fire. Losses mounted with every step, the attack lost steam and the men fell back. The incoming Confederate rifle fire was so intense that no one reached the bridge.[36]

Doctor Theodore Dimon of the Second Maryland watched from behind as his unit moved ahead to make the attack. He wrote, "The Regiment flanked off across some ploughed ground towards the bridge, the Colonel at the head, pulling down fences." The Marylanders lost 67 of their 162 men in the effort.[37]

"The Regiment…all alone, was stopped to throw down the fence on the other side of the field. Duryea [the Colonel] had just thrown down the last rail and, as he looked back, he saw the Regiment shrinking and elbowing out under this tremendous fire and just ready to break. The ploughed furrows were thickly dotted with fallen men." Colonel J. Eugene Duryea yelled above the noise, "What the hell are you doing there? Straighten out that line there, forward." Dimon saw that "the line straightened, like straightening your arm, and on it went for the bridge."[38]

The Forty-Eighth Pennsylvania and the Ninth New Hampshire fired a great deal of their ammunition during the assault as they provided covering fire. By the time they went forward later in the day, these troops were nearly out of cartridges. Captain James Wren, commanding Company B, Forty-Eighth Pennsylvania, met a soldier from the Sixth New Hampshire with his finger shot off but still with a full cartridge box of forty rounds. Wren told his compatriot,

> *Now you bite the ends off these Cartridges & I will fire them Cartridges of yours, & I lay down my sword & took up the musket and fired his musket until it got so hot in the Barrel I Could not hold it & laid it down & by this time thear was plenty of spare guns & I picked up another & fired until the Command was given to Cease firing. We then Charged the Bridge & Carried it & drove the enemy before us under a heavy fire of grape and shell.*[39]

During the assault on the bridge, Wren noticed a Confederate firing from behind a tree at the bridge's west side. Three times this man fired on Wren, the ball passing just over his head. Wren waited for him and fired when he appeared again but missed. Then, when he rose again, Wren fired and saw him fall. After crossing the bridge, Wren found the dead man lying on the ground.[40]

Although successfully repelling the attacks, the Georgia defenders were running low on ammunition themselves. Colonel William R. Holmes of the Second Regiment went to get some but was shot and killed instantly. Four soldiers tried to retrieve his body but were fired on; two of them were hit, and they abandoned the effort. Holmes was killed about half an hour before the bridge fell, at around twelve thirty. The incoming fire was so intense that three more balls struck his lifeless body.[41]

Toombs reported five separate attacks at bridge (there were actually three), but from his vantage point, he might have elevated skirmishing and maneuvering by Union troops across the creek to an attack. He notes in his report that he asked for reinforcements but could not get any, something that division commander D.R. Jones does not mention.[42]

Throughout the day, Union troops noted that the incoming artillery included not just shells but also railroad iron and other metal scraps, perhaps a reflection of a shortage of proper ammunition among the Confederates. A soldier in the Ninth New Hampshire noted that near the bridge, one piece of iron whizzed by his head and struck the ground, rolling end over end. After another piece of iron flew by, a German-born officer shouted, "*Mein Gott!* We shall see a blacksmith's shop to come next."[43]

McClellan sent another messenger urging Burnside to get his corps across the bridge, and Burnside sent an order directly to General Samuel Sturgis. Frustrated, Burnside ordered Sturgis to "carry the bridge at all hazards." With Nagle's brigade having failed, Colonel Edward Ferrero's brigade led the next attack, again under Cox's direct supervision. The two Fifty-Firsts, New York and Pennsylvania, made ready to charge over the dead and wounded from the previous two failed attacks. How well Burnside and Cox coordinated this attack is not recorded, but it seems Burnside was stepping in and out of the chain of command.[44]

Here one of the most infamous and enduring stories of the entire war emerges: that of the Fifty-First Pennsylvania demanding their whiskey ration in return for taking the bridge. Though the story is often repeated in histories, it has never been established exactly what they did to lose their ration or even if it was ever restored afterward. Only one source, the regimental history written by Thomas Parker, even mentions it.

What is clear is that previously, when stationed in New Bern, North Carolina, the unit was issued whiskey, as were all troops, which was thought to counteract unhealthy air and water in that region. The Pennsylvanians

Map of troop positions at 11:00 a.m. *Hal Jespersen.*

were a little too eager to enjoy their medicine. Parker noted, "Whiskey was in town and the boys did get it—much as they wanted and more than they needed." Colonel Edward Ferrero remarked on their ability to find spiritous liquors: "Were my men to be cast on an island where whiskey was never known to have been, and they allowed to run at will, scarcely a man but what would come into camp with his canteen full, even if they would have to rend rocks asunder searching for it."[45]

Yet their whiskey ration was restored before departing North Carolina. It must have been revoked again before Antietam, but the records on any incident are silent. Perhaps their transfer from the unhealthy coastal area no longer necessitated having it. Did the Pennsylvanians get their whiskey after Antietam? Historical records do not say.[46]

To support this next effort, artillerymen brought a light howitzer from Captain Seth Simmond's Kentucky battery down to the clearing before the bridge so it could fire directly onto the far side of the creek. The only Kentucky troops present in the battle (and some of the few serving in the east), they played a prominent but little-known role here. As the troops on the high ground near the bridge began to lay down covering fire, the howitzer's crew fired double charges of canister at the Confederates.[47]

Colonel Edward Ferrero sent an orderly and told him to "take the two Fifty-Firsts" and seize the bridge. "It is General Burnside's special request," Ferrero yelled to the two regiments, "that the two Fifty-Firsts take that bridge. Will you do it?"

Quickly, the teetotaling Corporal Lewis Patterson replied, "Will you give us our whiskey, Colonel, if we take it?"

Ferrero answered affirmatively before asking again, "Will you take it?"

"Yes," the men shouted back.

Parker recorded that Ferrero said,

> *Yes, by God, you shall all have as much as you want, if you take the bridge. I don't mean the whole brigade, but you two regiments shall have just as much as you want, if it is in the commissary, or I have to send to New York to get it, and pay for it out of my own private purse; that is, if I live to see you through it. Will you take it?*[48]

Captain William Bolton, who led the Fifty-First Pennsylvania's Company A, wrote in his diary that before assaulting the bridge, "Ferrero in a loud clear voice called for [Col. John F.] Hartranft," who commanded the regiment, "and in a voice we all could hear, [Ferrero] commanded 'Burnside orders you to take the 51st P.V. and storm the bridge.'" He described how they ran forward "through a perfect hell of shot and shell."[49]

Major Edwin Schall of the regimental staff wrote that as the regiment began its advance,

> *There, by the roadside, stand Gen. Sturgis, and Gen. Ferrero. Says Gen. Sturgis as we pass, "If you take that bridge, you will accomplish one of the greatest feats of the war, and your name will be recorded in History." "We will do it," is the responding cry of the soldiers.*[50]

The two regiments charged in columns, reached the stone wall along creek at the bridge's entrance and returned fire on the Confederates. Colonel John Hartranft, leading the Fifty-First Pennsylvania, recalled,

> *As the regiment charged across, it was subject to a close, continued and deadly fire. Along the upper side of the road was a complete post and rail fence connecting with the upper wing-wall of the bridge. This was a serious obstacle.... Part of the command climbed over the fence and took possession of the lower wing-wall, which turned sufficiently down stream to afford some protection, and those getting to the center of the bridge were compelled to cross the bridge for shelter, and part took position behind the wall along the stream above the bridge. While the men replied to the fire of the enemy, I was at the end of the upper wing-wall and had the two panels of fence nearest the bridge torn down.*[51]

After a short time, Captain William Allebaugh of the Fifty-First Pennsylvania's color guard jumped up and led the small detachment up to the bridge under heavy fire. Several fell before setting foot on the span, but Allebaugh rushed over with five men of the color guard behind him. These six were the first Union troops over the bridge. The rest of the Fifty-First Pennsylvania and Fifty-First New York followed quickly. By this time, Confederate defenders were running uphill from their rifle pits to get away.[52]

Theodore Fogle of the Second Georgia observed that fellow soldier Johnny Slade had fired nearly all his cartridges when he stood up to see where his last shot had gone. At that moment, a ball passed through the third finger of his right hand and into his body. The bullet exited his back, having pierced several organs, and Slade died that night.[53]

Colonel Henry L. Benning wrote that he ordered the defenders back once the bridge was lost and Rodman's troops crossed the creek. He also noted that they were out of ammunition, having been firing for about four hours. Lieutenant Farquhar McCrimmon of the Twentieth Georgia and sixteen privates were captured on the heights above the bridge as the Fifty-First Pennsylvania and New York swarmed over. Their captors were caught up in the heat of the moment, frustrated after enduring the Georgian's rifle fire for so long and ready to shoot them when a colonel rode up and intervened, ensuring the prisoners were sent to the rear.[54]

Toombs ordered the Georgians to regroup on the ridge overlooking the forty-acre cornfield on the far right of the army, where important events would take place in a few hours. But at the moment, it was a convenient and militarily sound spot to make a stand. From here, the Georgians fell back to the Harpers Ferry Road, where it was discovered that Company D of the Second, the Burke Sharpshooters, was missing. Amid the noise and confusion, they had not heard the order to retreat from their position

The charge across the bridge. *Battles and Leaders*.

overlooking the creek near the bridge. Lieutenant Perry went to find them, and they eventually rejoined the unit.[55]

Lieutenant Colonel Kearse of the Fiftieth Georgia, realizing that Union troops had crossed behind his line at Snavely's Ford, ordered his men to fall back. They retreated a few hundred yards to the high ground in their rear, near Otto Lane, and then back to rejoin the whole command.[56]

The Second Georgia lost half its men defending the bridge, losing forty-two of its ninety-seven soldiers, as well as its commander, Colonel Holmes. The Twentieth Georgia ran out of ammunition. The Second Georgia fell back and reunited with the Fiftieth Georgia and the attached South Carolina company. Private Theodore Fogle of the Second Georgia wrote that they had so few soldiers that officers helped load and fire rifles. As the Federals stormed the bridge, Major Harris, his cousin, ordered them to fall back.[57]

As the Georgians fell back, Fogle had to leave his wounded friend Spivey, who was shot through the knee and unable to walk. He wrote, "It was the hardest thing I ever had to do to leave him but we had to double quick to save ourselves from being taken prisoner."[58]

By this time, the Fifteenth and Seventeenth Georgia arrived from their mission to guard supply wagons and took position along the Harpers Ferry

Road while the Second and Twentieth Georgia went to the rear to replenish their cartridge boxes. Private Ivy Dugan of the Fifteenth Georgia wrote that as they arrived at the battlefield, they began to be shelled. One explosion killed the color-bearer, tore the flag and injured several other men. Toombs ordered Benning to move to the right rear to rest. Then Benning got orders to move to the left, along the road to Sharpsburg, putting his troops in the center of the Confederate line along the Harpers Ferry Road. The men moved at double-quick pace past a cornfield to get there, linking up with the rest of the division.[59]

In the meantime, Colonel Robert Potter came up with his regiment, the Fifty-First New York, and formed along the fence to the south of the bridge. He wrote,

> *The fence afforded little protection and the 51st New York was losing heavily. This also impelled me to arouse my regiment to another effort to cross. Passing through the opening in the fence with the colors and a few officers and men on to the Bridge, and they passing, I called on the regiment to follow. While thus engaged, Col. Potter came up, likewise calling to his regiment. Both regiments responded promptly, and passing rapidly over the bridge, the 51st Pennsylvania filed to the right on the roadway and the 51st New York to the left.*[60]

When the flag bearers reached the center of the bridge, the Confederates ceased firing and began falling back. This attack succeeded with a combination of rapid movement, covering fire and artillery support. The two Fifty-Firsts charged rapidly and only briefly paused at the bridge's west side before surging ahead; it all happened fairly quickly. Colonel John Hartranft stood at the stone wall near the edge of the bridge, waved his hat in the air and yelled out, "Come on boys, for I can't haloo any more!" He became hoarse and sat exhausted on the edge of the bridge once the two regiments were over. Both units had depleted their ammunition; some men had only a few cartridges left.[61]

Doctor Theodore Dimon, watching the charge, noted that the two Fifty-Firsts charged at a run through the gap between the Second Maryland and Sixth New Hampshire. As they crossed, the Fifty-First Pennsylvania got "jammed" at the bridge's entrance. He saw Colonel Robert Potter jump on the wooden parapet on the bridge's wall and urge the Fifty-First New York through the Pennsylvanians, swearing as he did so.[62]

The Twenty-First and Thirty-Fifth Massachusetts followed swiftly over behind the two Fifty-Firsts. On the slope beyond, much of the Second

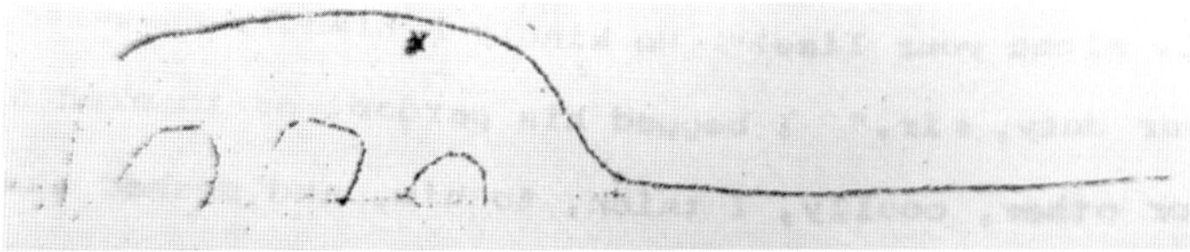

Bridge sketch by John Hudson, Thirty-Fifth Massachusetts. *Antietam Park Library.*

Georgia's color guard was killed, and Lieutenant Colonel Holmes's body was found lying five steps behind his dead men. The Twenty-First Massachusetts had used most of its ammunition, so its troops paused to collect cartridges from the dead and wounded before pressing over the bridge.[63]

The Thirty-Fifth Massachusetts, a brand-new unit, made their way over the bridge next, stepping over the dead and wounded on the road and the span. As they reached the far shore, they began intermixing with some of the men of the two Fifty-Firsts. All three units began scooping up Confederate prisoners who had been too slow to get away, some in their rifle pits, others dropping from trees where they had been firing down onto the bridge. Some waved dirty white rags in token of surrender.[64]

The Thirty-Fifth Massachusetts moved up the steep hill and over rail fences beyond, finally reaching the brow of the hill. To their right were the two Fifty-Firsts. Incoming artillery fire forced them to fall back behind a rail fence, and even some Union shells landed among them on the hill west of the bridge. Colonel Sumner Carruth waved his hat in an effort to halt the friendly fire and yelled to his color-bearer, "Unfurl those colors and wave them!" The unit had no United States flag, only the white banner of Massachusetts. Thankfully, the incoming fire from the rear stopped, and they settled down to await events.[65]

After the war, several men of the Thirty-Fifth Massachusetts wrote about the nerve-racking wait under fire:

> *At such times men's characters reveal themselves: the religiously disposed bends his thoughts on Heaven; the less devout watches the ants busy as usual at their never-ending labors, and wishes he could be as small as they for a few hours; while the more thoughtless cuts his tobacco and enjoys its soothing influence.*

The men ate their hardtack, and Colonel Carruth sent a detachment down to the creek to fill canteens.[66]

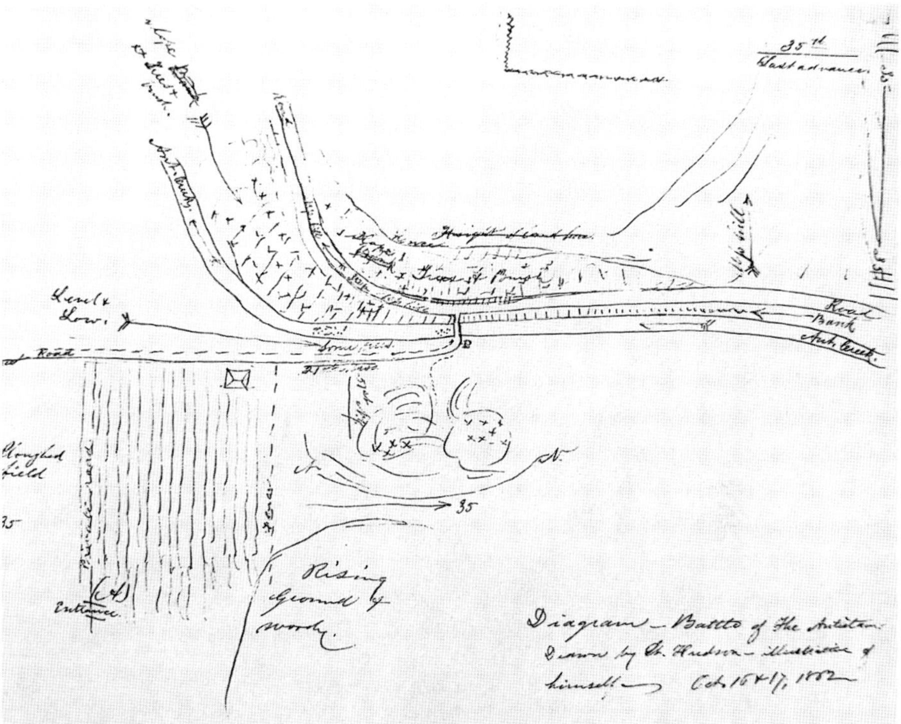

Map of the bridge area by John Hudson, Thirty-Fifth Massachusetts. *Antietam Park Library.*

Colonel Enoch Q. Fellows and the Ninth New Hampshire watched the successful attack from the heights east of the bridge. Fellows was sporting a palm leaf hat for better shade from the sun than a military-issue kepi. On seeing the two Fifty-Firsts make it across, he shouted, "Forward Ninth New Hampshire! Follow the old palm leaf!" Waving his nonregulation hat, he led them forward in the wake of the two lead regiments. Once across the bridge, the New Englanders went directly up the bluff beyond it, moving to Otto's Lane. Behind them was the Ninth New York (Hawkins' Zouaves). Here they encountered a worse enemy than Confederate troops: a startled cow charged into their midst, causing confusion and scattering the men for a few minutes.[67]

While engaging in long-range rifle fire with Tombs's men to their front, Private Wesley Simonds of the Ninth New Hampshire had the sole of one shoe ripped off by a bullet. He paused to take off the mangled shoe and continued fighting with only one shoe on. A comrade saw this and said, "Simonds, what are you going 'round barefoot for, when there's plenty of shoes lying 'round here, doing nobody any good?" He replied, "Sure enough, strange I never thought of that," and found a shoe that fit perfectly.[68]

At about the same time, Captain Andrew J. Stone and Private Herman A. Clement of the Ninth New Hampshire were standing side by side. Stone saw a shell flying toward them and yelled, "Drop!" Clement went to the ground, and the projectile went over both of them, burying itself in the ground beyond them. Nearby were brothers W.W. and J.H. Humphreys, one right-handed and the other a southpaw. The right-handed one lost his right thumb, and the left-handed one had his left thumb shot off.[69]

Once the Union troops were over the bridge, events moved rapidly and simultaneously. At about the same time Sturgis's men carried the bridge, General Isaac Rodman's troops crossed the creek to the south at Snavely's Ford, and Toombs's position became untenable. Having used a lot of their ammunition in the assault, Ferrero's brigade was low by the time they reached the other side and deployed. This would come back to haunt the Ninth Corps later. Having taken the bridge and forced the defenders back, Burnside's corps now paused and lost the initiative. The delay was necessary to resupply the troops, and the narrow width of the bridge itself did not allow for quick movement.[70]

The two Fifty-Firsts were relieved. They moved back from the front line and rested and stacked arms near the bridge's west side. Some men began making coffee. Thomas Parker of the Fifty-First Pennsylvania noted, "While the two regiments remained at the bridge the enemy kept up a terrible cannonading; solid shot, shell, case-shot, grape &., rained down on the devoted bridge like hail." Colonel Ferrero was sitting on the wall of the bridge when a shell struck about fifteen inches below him, tearing part of the wall away but leaving him unharmed.[71]

Cox noted that the three efforts to take the bridge (Crook's misguided assault, the Second Maryland and the Sixth New Hampshire and the two Fifty-Firsts) were all done "as closely following each other as possible." He stated, "The lulls in the fighting had been short, and only to prepare new efforts." This is probably true, for if the first assault went forward around ten o'clock in the morning and the last succeeded around one o'clock in the afternoon, each effort took about forty-five minutes. This was just enough time for the previous assaulting force to fall back and the next one to prepare to go forward.[72]

The Forty-Eighth Pennsylvania crossed the bridge and made their way to the front. Under intense artillery fire, they crawled up to the crest at

Otto's Lane, where they found the Fifty-First Pennsylvania lying flat on ground firing but low on ammunition. The Forty-Eighth came up behind them and relieved them, taking their place on the line, and the Fifty-First moved to the rear. The day was warm, and rifles got hot in the soldiers' hands. The Forty-Eighth began to run low on ammunition and had to pull back by evening to replenish their supply.[73]

Once over the bridge, Captain James Wren sent three companies of the Forty-Eighth Pennsylvania out in advance as skirmishers, and they met troops coming up from Snavely's Ford, then fell back to rejoin the unit. Gradually officers began to realize that they held the ground above the bridge and began to get the lay of the land. They found Confederate dead among some haystacks that had been roasted when the hay caught fire from incoming shells. A sword recovered from a dead officer was found to have been taken from Lieutenant J.W. Shoemaker of the Fourth Pennsylvania Reserves two weeks earlier at Second Manassas.

David Davis found a dead Confederate's haversack with johnnycakes (cornbread) in it and began eating them. A fellow soldier said he couldn't eat anything from a dead man's haversack. "Damn 'em man, the Johnny is dead, but the Johnnycakes is no Dead," said Davis. Finding the body of Colonel William R. Holmes of the Second Georgia in a ditch, a Pennsylvania soldier took his gold watch, while his boots were divided among two other privates.[74]

Captain Oliver Bosbyshell of the Forty-Eighth Pennsylvania followed over the bridge and up the hill. Along the way, he saw a dead Georgia officer. Private Clem Evans took his sword, rejoined the command and reported that the officer was actually not quite dead but no longer needed his sword. Evans later regretted taking the trophy, finding it a burden to carry, and offered it to Bosbyshell, who gladly accepted it.[75]

Joseph Gould of the Forty-Eighth noted,

> *The rebels opened a terrific fire of grape, canister and spherical case from several batteries in front, causing us to shelter ourselves under the hill. 'Twas not long before the infantry became engaged, and at 5 P.M., we were ordered forward to support the 51st Pennsylvania Volunteers. We hurried up the hill (taking our position immediately in the rear of the 51st, lying flat on the ground. The artillery firing was terrible, and the range awfully accurate. The 51st's ammunition giving out, we crawled up into its place, while it took ours, determined to support us. Finding our batteries could not get a position to support us, we were ordered to retreat, which we did in*

> *good order, to the bridge, where fresh ammunition was obtained, when we returned and slept on the battlefield.*[76]

Charles A. Cuffel of the regiment noted that they advanced west to a stone wall at Otto Lane, with a ravine in front. The Ninth Corps' artillery had moved across the bridge to deploy on the high ground to support the infantry advance. Behind the Forty-Eighth Pennsylvania, Durell's Battery (Pennsylvania Independent Battery D) deployed and began firing over their heads with their six ten-pound Parrot guns.[77]

From their vantage point, the Pennsylvanians sent out skirmishers to the front, and the entire regiment could watch the subsequent charge of the Ninth New York. Bosbyshell wrote, "The rebel artillery made it woefully hot for the skirmishers on this open hill top, and the line got under over behind a large hay-stack, where the enemy's operations could be observed with more comfort and safety."[78]

All the while, Cox and Burnside hoped to hear from Rodman about his crossing downstream, but so far, there was no news. In the meantime, orders from McClellan arrived, noting the urgency of attacking and getting across the creek. By this point, the fighting had long ended at the northern end of the battlefield, and in the center, the Sunken Road was in Union hands, but fighting sputtered out there as well. From here on, the only major action would be in the south in the Ninth Corps' sector.

The bridge was secured around one o'clock, at about the same time that troops forded Antietam Creek downstream at Snavely's Ford. Yet those who had crossed in Sturgis's division were low on ammunition, having fired nearly all their cartridges in the first three assaults to take the bridge. Cox asked Burnside to replace Sturgis's division with Willcox's division and Crook's brigade. By the time the fresh troops crossed the creek, deployed and prepared to advance, it was around three o'clock. The single-lane bridge and the narrow road on either side of it made moving troops, ammunition and supplies time-consuming. In addition, the bluffs that Willcox's men were forced to climb were almost ninety degrees in places. Some of the men had to grab hold of roots and branches just to pull themselves up. The ground at the bridge was steep enough, but Willcox's men, especially Colonel Benjamin Christ's brigade, had even steeper bluffs to climb in order to prepare for their late afternoon advance.[79]

A two-hour delay seems absurd to modern readers, but it must be remembered that orders were being delivered verbally by messenger, which involved finding the recipient. Units were spread out, and no one knew the local roads or the lay of the land. Troops took time to form and begin marching. And what made it all worse were the hilly terrain, the narrow road and the bridge bottleneck. No one in the Union army had been here before; no one knew the terrain or shortcuts.

Cox, overseeing the operation directly on the west side of the creek, advised Burnside of the need to swap out the troops before the advance could continue, noting that "it was imperative that they should be freshly supplied before entering into another engagement." He continued, "This was done as rapidly as was practicable, where everything had to pass down the steep hill road and through so narrow a defile as the bridge." Burnside himself was on the west bank of the creek at the bridge to help direct traffic. This was a dangerous place to be, as incoming artillery fire was dropping in as the wagons delivered cartridges at the west end of the bridge.[80]

Lieutenant Matthew Graham, wounded and on his way to the rear, described the scene when he reached the bridge and saw artillery and wagons crossing: "The rebels opened fire with as much vim and energy as they had shown earlier in the day. There was a rush to cross, each driver trying to get ahead of all the others. They became jammed on the bridge."[81]

The Fifty-First Pennsylvania was resupplied with ammunition and advanced to the brow of the hill at Otto's Lane, overlooking a large cornfield. They could see the Confederates on the high ground ahead of them and lay down to avoid the incoming artillery fire. One soldier noted that shells were coming in just three feet above their heads. At about two o'clock in the afternoon, the Forty-Fifth Pennsylvania of Welsh's brigade relieved them.

Swapping troops out under fire is a difficult task. "The men began to leave separately and in pairs," wrote Thomas Parker of the Fifty-First Pennsylvania, "some sliding down the hill on their backs, feet foremost, some on their stomachs, some head foremost, some rolled down, some few jumped to their feet and ran with their utmost speed, while others lingered for a more favorable opportunity."[82]

The Sixth New Hampshire halted on the crest beyond the bridge and exchanged long-range fire with the enemy in the distance. Sergeant Rand of Company K found himself next to W.W. French of Company B, behind a tree, firing. Rand asked French to load for him, and he would fire, knowing Rand was a good shot. French agreed, and once ready, Rand stepped to the side of a tree to fire but was instantly hit in the forehead. His body fell onto French, and both rolled downhill. French managed to get out from under Rand's body and made his way back up to the tree, careful not to get out from its cover.[83]

Crossing the bridge, the Seventy-Ninth New York noted the numerous Union dead in front of and on the span. This was a colorful unit of Highlanders, wearing tartan trousers and bonnets. The New Yorkers moved up the road and formed on the extreme right of the Ninth Corps in a double skirmish line. A thousand yards away, they saw the Confederates of Evans's and Jenkins's brigades. As soon as the Seventy-Ninth entered the open ground of a plowed field north of the Sherrick Farm, the New Yorkers began receiving artillery fire. They advanced to within three hundred yards of the Confederate guns. Here they were joined on their right by the Second United States, a Fifth Corps unit that had crossed at the middle bridge. In their advanced position, the New Yorkers could pick off some of the Confederate gunners on the prominent hill to their front. They held this advanced position until their ammunition ran out, and then the Highlanders withdrew.[84]

Back near the bridge, Captain John Griswold's corpse still lay on the west bank from the Eleventh Connecticut's first attack hours earlier. Once Union troops passed by and secured the area, his comrades could retrieve his body.

A soldier in the Fifty-First Pennsylvania noted that after securing the bridge, two Confederates were actually seen under the span, cooking over a fire. Soldiers seized the two men and confiscated their frying pan and food. Another Confederate was found hiding in a tree, so well concealed he was almost not noticed. Hoping to remain unseen and get away, the discovered soldier was brought down and captured.[85]

At about the time the two Fifty-Firsts secured the bridge, Colonel George Crook's Twenty-Eighth Ohio found a crossing north of the bridge, "not over knee deep." His other two units, the Eleventh and Thirty-Sixth, followed over to the west bank.[86]

John Hudson of the Thirty-Fifth Massachusetts noted the terrain over which his unit advanced after crossing the bridge: "The opposite bank of the stream was 8 to 10 ft. higher than the water, the road beyond it very narrow and bounded on the farther side by a bank 6 to 12 feet high as steep as that rocky formation would lie if dug away perpendicularly."[87]

It was indeed difficult terrain across which to move large bodies of troops and supplies, bottlenecked not only by the bridge but also the narrow roads on either side of it. With three of the four divisions of the corps now across at the bridge, the fourth also made its crossing downstream.

Chapter 2

IN SEARCH OF A FORD

One of the Union efforts that could have made a crucial difference if it was carried out earlier and more efficiently was crossing the creek at a ford downstream. Union forces' inability to find the ford or adequately scout the area on either side of the bridge for potential crossings was a major failure of this day.

General Isaac P. Rodman's division, along with Colonel Hugh Ewing's Ohio brigade of the Kanawha Division, participated in this time-consuming expedition, all the while under fire from the Georgians and South Carolinians on high ground across the stream who shadowed them as they advanced. They began around ten o'clock in the morning, and it would be nearly one o'clock in the afternoon when they successfully forded the creek.

Lieutenant Matthew Graham of the Ninth New York recalled that they took "what appeared to be an old wood-road" in their movement to find the ford. Lieutenant Henry B. Brinkerhoff of the Thirtieth Ohio recalled that it was a "zig zag march, behind hills and along ravines." Corporal George Merriman of the Sixteenth Connecticut wrote of the long search for a crossing, "We marched one way and another for nearly two hours."[88]

Rodman found the ford that he believed Duane had identified, but the banks were too steep, and it was covered by the enemy across the creek, so the column kept moving, looking for a better spot. Few details were recorded about this effort, so this was likely a process of checking the creek at favorable-looking spots, taking into account the banks, all while under fire of Confederates opposites them. With the help of an unnamed local guide, they finally found Snavely's Ford, a good crossing and possibly the

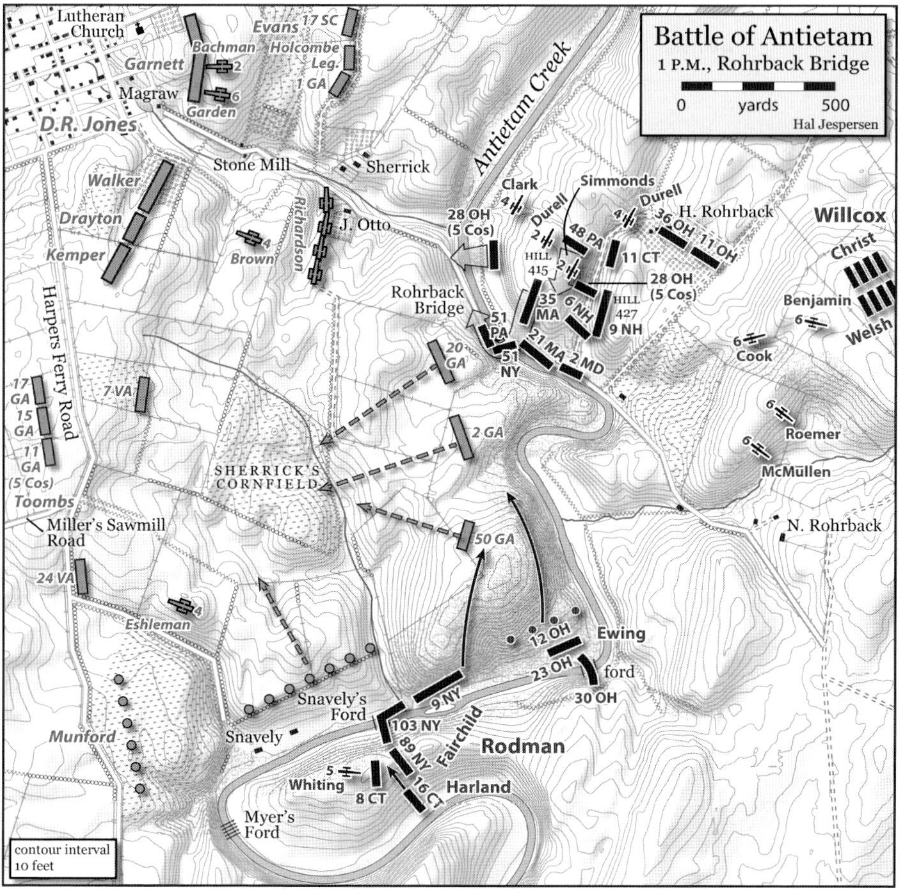

Map of troop positions at 1:00 p.m. *Hal Jespersen.*

one Duane had identified, or intended, for the troops to use. They had gone nearly two miles from the bridge, and the ford had steep ground above it to the northeast.[89]

Horace Williams with Company A, Eighth Connecticut was out in front searching for a crossing. On finding Snavely's Ford, the Eighth crossed, went uphill rapidly and saw the Confederates of Toombs's brigade falling back. Lieutenant Graham of the Ninth New York (Hawkins' Zouaves) notes, "When partly across we received the fire of a detachment was stationed behind a wall at the head of a ravine which opened up from the water towards our left front." The New Yorkers didn't return fire while in the stream but got across as quickly as possible. At least one man fell wounded while crossing.[90]

BRIGADIER-GENERAL ISAAC P. RODMAN, MORTALLY WOUNDED AT ANTIETAM. FROM A PHOTOGRAPH.

General Isssac P. Rodman. *Battles and Leaders.*

Charles Johnson of the Ninth New York was making entries into a notebook he carried in his pocket that day. He wrote, "After many dubious windings and turnings into the woods, we came to what appeared to be the rapids, and into this we plunged. Some Rebel sharpshooters discovered us and did not fail to scatter a few of their bullets from long range." They clambered up the steep cliff on the other side with "considerable difficulty." Having moved for hours and likely having no idea where they were in relation to the rest of the corps, an exasperated Johnson wrote, "God only knows where we will be before the sun goes down."[91]

How deep was the creek that day? It is an important question for this part of the battlefield. Numerous Union accounts note it was deep and a considerable obstacle. It seems the creek was higher than normal, and soldiers noted that it did rain the night before. Regardless of its depth, however, the banks in most places were steep, and on the west (the Confederate side of the creek), the ground rose steeply.[92]

Charles Johnson described the crossing as "hard work…scrambling up the face of an almost perpendicular cliff." A soldier in the Fourth Rhode Island noted that Snavely's Ford was "breast deep" when they splashed across. Another account described it as hip deep.[93]

A soldier in the Sixteenth Connecticut noted that the creek was shoulder deep, and another described it as waist deep. Captain Robert Kellogg of the Sixteenth called it "knee deep." Corporal George Merriman described it as "waist deep." A soldier in the Thirtieth Ohio called it "waist deep." David L. Thompson of the Ninth New York reported it was "waist deep." Writing thirty-two years later, Matthew Graham of the Ninth New York admitted his memory was foggy: "I do not remember how deep it was, but it was quite an effort to stem the stream." This would also have been much more challenging under fire. Perhaps the few statements that mention deep water were from men who happened to cross outside or on the edge of the ford or stumbled into a deep spot.[94]

Confederate defenders fired on the Union troops as they crossed from the nearby Snavely House and a stone wall above the creek. The Rhode

Islanders sent skirmishers forward, and the rest of the regiment followed up quickly Once across, the Fourth Rhode Island moved to the left, while Fairchild's New York regiments crossed and moved to the right. The men of the rookie Sixteenth Connecticut advanced to the top of the hill beyond the ford with the rest of their brigade and took what cover they could below the crest. A survivor noted that Confederate artillery "opened in all their fury, and seemed to shake the very earth under our feet." With the ground being torn up around them, the men could do little but lie down and hope for the best as shells burst overhead and fragments rained down among them. Here the unit lost twelve men, with no enemy in sight.[95]

George Allen of the Fourth Rhode Island's notes also mention incoming artillery fire, specifically grapeshot and shells. The shelling was accurate and unnerving to the men, who waited while the rest of Harland's brigade moved ahead.[96]

The Ninth New York attempted to climb the steep hill directly ahead of the ford but found "towering rocks" that they could not get over. The men broke up to the right and left, advancing to drive away the Confederate defenders above them. Lieutenant Matthew Graham wrote that "the ground was very

Snavely's Ford. *Author.*

rough and difficult and also very steep." General Rodman accompanied the New Yorkers uphill, walking on foot with them.[97]

One enduring question has been whether Ewing's Ohio brigade crossed at Snavely's Ford with Rodman's division or at a separate ford farther to the east (and closer to their starting point) at a sharp bend in the creek. Accounts from soldiers in the Ohio regiments confirm that they crossed here and not at Snavely's. This is possibly the ford that Rodman found earlier and rejected (and likely the one that Duane found the day before). The Twelfth Ohio waded across first, and the Thirtieth crossed last. This also took place around twelve thirty or one o'clock in the afternoon.[98]

Samuel Compton of the Twelfth Ohio noted, "The water came to my armpits and I had to hold my haversack and cartridge box over my head." How Ewing's troops found this ford, what made them decide to cross here and what they knew about Rodman's movement downstream remains unknown. Was this the ford Duane supposedly found? Again, it is impossible to say.[99]

The crossing was made under heavy Confederate artillery fire. Edward Henry of the Twenty-Third Ohio recalled, "One of the Thirtieth Ohio was shot through the leg with a sledgehammer....Horseshoes, doorknobs, buttons, and such like articles were taken out of our wounded."[100]

By three o'clock that Wednesday afternoon, the Ninth Corps had formed for its advance, with Willcox's division on the right, along the road to town; Rodman's on the left; and Scammon's and Sturgis's in reserve. The Sixteenth Connecticut and Fourth Rhode Island advanced on the far left to a cornfield (Sherrick's, or the forty-acre cornfield), and lay down. Captain Barber led Company H of the Sixteenth uphill in front as skirmishers.[101]

David L. Thompson of the Ninth New York recalled, "At the foot of the slope on the opposite side the line was formed and we moved up through the thin woods. Reaching the level we lay down behind a battery which seemed to have been disabled." The men were soaked from the waist down from the crossing.[102]

Lieutenant Graham of the Ninth wrote that Clark's Battery (Fourth U.S., Battery E) was nearby, but the incoming Confederate artillery fire was so accurate that they often stepped away from their guns. "The practice of the rebel artillerymen was something wonderful in its accuracy, they dropped shot and shell right into our line repeatedly. They kept the air fairly filled with missiles of almost every variety, from shrapnel to railroad iron." Posted in greater numbers and on higher ground, Southern artillery enjoyed a distinct advantage here.[103]

Company K of the Ninth New York was actually an artillery battery composed of five Dahlgren boat twelve-pound howitzers (two rifled, two smoothbore and one of unknown type). The guns were deployed to fire on the Confederates defending the ford, and after the infantry crossed, the guns entered the stream to ford the creek. Finding the ground beyond too difficult for the battery, the howitzers recrossed the stream and moved back to cross at the bridge, by now in Union hands. Near the span, they met General Burnside, who instructed the men to park the guns and take up their rifles.[104]

As Rodman's regiments advanced uphill, they deployed and rested, lying down for cover. They soon became aware that the bridge had been carried, meeting skirmishers from that direction. With friendly troops advancing on their right, they could turn their full attention to the enemy in their front. Incoming artillery fire increased, as the troops were well within range of the Confederate guns.[105]

A New Yorker from the Eighty-Ninth regiment noted that they were on the receiving end of "a blacksmith's shop, judging from the unearthly noise which it made screeching through the air." Observing the incoming artillery fire, a sergeant exclaimed, "I'll be hanged if I don't believe they are throwing wind-mills, by the racket they make."[106]

While he was waiting amid the men of the Ninth New York, a shell exploded between the head and horse of Captain Gardner, fragments landing all around; the horse had only a scratch on one leg. Another Confederate shell burst among the unit's six-man color guard, piercing the silk flag in many places, killing three and wounding four. The surviving corporal was thrown downhill but otherwise unhurt. Thirty-nine-year-old Lieutenant Colonel Edgar A. Kimball, commanding the Zouaves, waited anxiously, pacing up and down the line, and remarked that he felt he would be killed in the coming attack. General Rodman arrived and ordered forward one company of the Ninth New York as skirmishers; then the entire brigade advanced. It was about three thirty.[107]

The Confederate defense line began to take shape west of the bridge. Anchored on the hill on the Boonsboro Pike now occupied by Antietam National Cemetery, it ran along the high ground to the south. From left to right, the brigades of Garnett, Jenkins, Drayton, Kemper and Toombs fell into line. They had the advantage of high ground, numerous fences and stone walls and adequate artillery support.

Back at Harpers Ferry, General A.P. Hill's division had remained that morning to oversee the distribution of captured supplies and paroling of prisoners. General Lee sent an order for Hill to hurry to Sharpsburg and rejoin the army, and Hill quickly prepared his troops. General Maxcey Gregg's South Carolina brigade left first, marching by seven thirty in the morning. Civil War armies typically took a ten-minute break every hour, but Hill's troops took only a few breaks in their hurry to reach the battlefield. It was a quick but not breakneck pace, certainly not one of the longest or fastest of the war. The march has risen to legendary status due to the division's impact on the battle.

They heard the booming of artillery as they neared the Potomac River. Colonel James Lane noted that it was a "rapid and fatiguing march." The division crossed the Potomac at Pack Horse Ford (or Botelor's) at around two o'clock in the afternoon. William H. McLaurin of the Eighteenth North Carolina wrote of "our hard march from Harpers Ferry, wading the Potomac… our clothing saturated with water from the hips down." Straggling was rampant in these units that were already understrength and fatigued. The Thirty-Seventh North Carolina, for example, had only fifty men when it reached the field. A.P. Hill states in his report that the march was seventeen miles, but in reality, it was thirteen. Having made the march, the troops had to go straight into battle. Most Confederate accounts don't mention a hard or exhausting march.[108]

Confederate artillery from a hill just east of Sharpsburg where the modern National Cemetery stands continued to pummel the Union troops as they advanced from the bridge. The batteries here included the Madison Light Artillery (Louisiana) under Captain G.V. Moody, the Brooks (South Carolina) Battery led by Lieutenant William Elliot and the King William (Virginia) Artillery under Captain T.H. Carter. These batteries had the range of the bridge and the approaches to it. Although their fire was indirect, it was extremely accurate, and they made the crossing a hazardous place.

John Hudson of the Thirty-Fifth Massachusetts observed mules and wagons crossing the bridge amid shells and noted that the artillery of the "rebs" made "the bridge impassable to teams." He also observed other troops crossing and moving to the front, including the impressive Hawkins' Zouaves (Ninth New York), whom he called the "Zous" in a letter to his wife.[109]

Chapter 3

SURGING AHEAD

Events now happened nearly simultaneously, so to examine them in detail, they are covered in the next three chapters, but it should be remembered that they were concurrent and interrelated. Once the Union advance got underway, problems developed immediately. Confederate artillery fire was intense, and accounts note its strength and accuracy. The Ninth Corps had two divisions of two brigades each advancing, meaning that four brigades were deployed to cover an area nearly a mile wide.

None advanced in tandem, partially because of the hilly terrain, which impeded movement and blocked vision, but also as a result of tenacious Confederate defenders. Southern units used the difficult agricultural landscape of the Otto and Sherrick farms (including structures, orchards and stone walls) to contest the Union advance on the road directly leading to Sharpsburg. To the left, or south, the brigades of Colonel Edward Harland and Colonel Harrison Fairchild also advanced unevenly. It was about three o'clock, or a little after, when the Ninth Corps lurched forward. The stage was now set for the final Union attack of the day at Antietam, though no one knew that yet. Civil War rifles had a range of about half a mile, so as they advanced, the Union troops would have been in range as soon as they crested the high ground beyond the bridge, east of Otto Lane.

While it is easy to second guess and criticize from a modern perspective, there seems to be plenty of blame for Union failures here to go around. Division commanders Orlando Willcox and Isaac Rodman could have

Map of troop positions at 3:00 p.m. *Hal Jespersen.*

coordinated their advance. Generals Jacob Cox and Ambrose Burnside could have also overseen the operation better and sent staff officers to ensure communication and coordination. As it was, the advance was spread over too wide a front, and no consideration was given to the fact that there were inexperienced units among the advancing troops. For example, the rookie Sixteenth Connecticut ended up on the left flank, nearly alone, with disastrous results. Difficult terrain that had not been scouted was also a major factor.

In their final attack, the Ninth Corps was occupying an area that two corps should have covered. By way of comparison, most of three Union corps fought over an area about the same size in the northern area of the battlefield that morning. The wide front meant that the Ninth Corps dispersed its units and had few in reserve to exploit a breakthrough or cover a retreat. The terrain was also more challenging here than anywhere else on the battlefield.

General Orlando B. Willcox's division moved beyond the bridge against General Thomas Drayton's brigade, whom they had fought at Fox's Gap three days before, as well as on Henry House Hill at Second Manassas two weeks ago. Ironically, they would meet again at Spotsylvania in 1864.

Willcox advanced on the town, while Crook's brigade of the Kanawha Division supported Wilcox's troops. To the left, or south, General Isaac P. Rodman's two brigades advanced, with Colonel Ewing's in support. General Samuel Sturgis's division, having been involved in two of the earlier attacks on the bridge, was held in reserve on the crest above the bridge.[110]

Willcox's division had Colonel Benjamin Christ's brigade on the right, north of the road that led to Sharpsburg, and Colonel Thomas Welsh's on the left. A section of artillery (two guns) advanced simultaneously in the road. Christ's brigade moved faster, having the advantage of tree cover and ground that protected them. A section of artillery moved with them in the road as they advanced. To their left, Welsh's troops moved a bit more slowly but soon caught up. Sturgis's troops, who had done most of the assaults on the bridge, were in position in reserve.[111]

Colonel Benjamin Christ, commanding the right brigade of Willcox's division, noted that after crossing the bridge, he deployed the Seventy-Ninth New York as skirmishers, with the Fiftieth Pennsylvania, Twenty-Eighth Massachusetts and Seventeenth Michigan in the rear of a cornfield on the right of the road. All the while, they were under heavy artillery fire. Without support on their left, they advanced against General Nathan Evans's brigade on the high ground beyond the Sherrick farm.[112]

Christ himself was at the head of the Fiftieth Pennsylvania, carrying the unit's state flag and urging the men forward, "amidst the whistling bullet and howling shells. The brigade, on the right of the Ninth Corps, was ahead of Welsh's to their left and the Fifth Corps on their right. At the crest of the hill, they lay down for cover.[113]

The terrain was hilly, the road in a deep valley. Christ's three regiments (Twenty-Eighth Massachusetts, Fiftieth Pennsylvania, Seventeenth Michigan) faced a large, plowed field in front of the Sherrick farm complex. In addition to the large brick house were a detached kitchen, smokehouse, corncrib and barn. These buildings sheltered Confederates, who also occupied an orchard just north of the home. The ground sloped up farther to the west and crested at the hill where the National Cemetery now stands.

The imposing brick house with its stone foundation had been built in the 1830s. The Sherricks were early settlers to the area; Joseph Sherrick Jr. and his wife owned the property in 1862 and worshiped at the nearby Dunker Church. By 1860, the couple was renting the farm to Leonard Emmert, who was there at the time of the battle.[114]

Like many other parts of the field, the entire area of Willcox's advance was under Confederate artillery fire, and for most of the advance, his men would be in range of troops from the Seventeenth South Carolina and Holcomb Legion (South Carolina) at the Sherrick and Otto farms, though the defenders' visibility was limited by the hills ahead of them. Although they had few infantry troops, the Confederates had adequate artillery support here, with nine batteries supporting Jones's division prior to the arrival of A.P. Hill's division.

General Richard Garnett's brigade was posted on a prominent hill just east of the town (where the National Cemetery is now located) to face the advancing Fifth Corps. Garnett fell back to assist Jones's other brigades at a stone wall as they faced pressure from Willcox's advance, led by skirmishers from the Seventy-Ninth New York.[115]

Crossing the bridge and moving up behind Willcox's division was Colonel George Crook's brigade of the Kanawha Division. Taking position behind Wilcox in the valley of the road along the creek was the Eleventh Ohio. An account from one if its soldiers described the terrain here west of the bridge: "On the other side the country was much broken."[116]

General Micah Jenkins's brigade (this day led by Lieutenant Colonel Joseph Walker) moved forward four hundred yards from its initial position on Cemetery Hill, just east of Sharpsburg. From left to right were the First, Fifth and Sixth South Carolina; the Palmetto Sharpshooters; and the Second South Carolina Rifles. They deployed in an apple orchard overlooking the road that ran into town "under a heavy fire of artillery and small arms." The South Carolinians charged at Christ's troops, who were behind a fence. Then, as the Federals advanced up the road toward the town, Walker turned his unit into line parallel with a ravine and the road to Sharpsburg, firing into the flank of Welsh's men. The First South Carolina began the battle with only 106 men and by day's end had only 16 left.[117]

Sergeant Frank M. Mixson of the First South Carolina wrote about their time in Sherrick's apple orchard: "It seemed as if they had placed all the cannon *in the world* up there; it was certainly the heaviest and most terrific artillery firing during the entire war." He continued,

> *We got in position on the hill in rear of an old plank fence and were told not to fire a shot till ordered to do so. While lying behind the fence the Yankees were making their charge and coming down the opposite hill in as pretty a line as on dress parade. In front of us, and about midway, there was a stone fence in another apple orchard. The Yankees were making for this fence.*
>
> *Our batteries were on the hill above us and were responding all they could.... We were ordered up the hill to protect our batteries, the enemy were charging them. We went up the hill at a double quick. Our regiment was on the left of the brigade and we were going left in front, which put us to the front. I was trotting by the side of Maj. Livingston amid a furor of bursting shells. About half way up the hill Maj. Livingston called to me saying "Lead on Frank, I am wounded." I called to Capt. Knotts, who was the senior Captain present, and told him to take command of the regiment. We got in position on the hill in rear of a plank fence and were told not to fire a shot till ordered to do so. While lying behind the fence the Yankees were making their charge and coming down the opposite hill in as pretty a line as on dress parade. In front of us, and about midway, there was a stone fence in another apple orchard. The Yankees were making for this fence, and as I said before, were moving on it at a double quick.... The old captain commanding our batteries had shot himself out of balls, and all his horses being killed, he ordered his men to cut off the trace chains. With these he loaded his pieces and fired. It seemed that as the chains reached the ranks they spread themselves out full length and cut their way broadside through. The old captain jumped up, yelled, and ordered another load, with about the same result. This was done several times, and finally the column began to waver and weaken. At this point a Yankee colonel rode to the front with drawn sword and rallied his men, who were about to give way. Just then I said to Kite Folk... "Let us shoot him." I picked up a gun lying near me and Kite and I put our guns through the fence and fired together. The colonel fell and was carried from the field. The enemy fell back, but very soon came again.*

A stone fence stood equal distance between the Union and Confederate infantry. Both charged, but as Mixson put it, "We won the race," and the Southerners fell in behind the barrier, with the Union troops just fifteen steps away. They retired, leaving many killed and wounded.[118]

Colonel William H. Withington of the Seventeenth Michigan "walked around amongst us at the battle the bullets flying all around him—he kept Shouting to us to fire low and give it to them." Sixteen-year-old Private

William Brearley of the Seventeenth left a detailed account. This was a new unit, having only joined the army in August and fought at South Mountain three days earlier. Brearley noted,

> *It was rather Strange music to hear balls scream within an inch of my head. I had a bullet strike me on the top of the head just as I was going to fire and a piece of Shell struck my foot—a ball hit my finger and another hit my thumb I concluded they meant me. The rebels played the mischief with us by raising a U.S. flag. We were ordered not to fire and as soon as we went forward they opened an awful fire from their batteries on us we were ordered to fall back about ½ miles....*
>
> *We rushed onto them every man for himself—all loading & firing as fast as he could see a rebel to Shoot at—at last the rebels began to get over the wall to the rear and run for the woods, the firing increased tenfold then it sounded like the rolls of thunder—and all the time every man shouting as loud as he could—I got rather more excited than I wish to again.*[119]

Captain E.B. Cantey, commanding the brigade's Sixth South Carolina, went down with four gunshot wounds as they charged to the stone wall at east side of an orchard. Darling Patterson, color-bearer of the First South Carolina, ran ahead with the flag flying, inspiring the others. Reaching the orchard, he stuck the flag into the ground.[120]

Having taken the fence, the South Carolinians were isolated and too far in front of their support. A Georgia captain arrived to warn them that the other Confederate troops had pulled back. Orderly Sergeant Frank Mixson yelled out to his men, "First South Carolina retreat," and led them back. As they withdrew, they had to run around the head of the advancing Forty-Fifth Pennsylvania, which nearly cut them off. When the Sixth South Carolina stopped to regroup, eighteen-year-old Sergeant Major Jim Hagood took over as commander, Cantey being wounded. Company E was down to one man, and Company had F none. "So, you see," wrote Mixson, "we were right badly used up."[121]

Colonel Welsh's four regiments faced more challenging terrain, having to cross hills and navigate through woods south of the road. The Otto farm and orchard provided cover to the Confederates five hundred yards away, and beyond that lay a series of ridges and open ground, leading up to the edge of town. Lumm's stone mill and a nearby orchard offered the enemy more protection and another rallying point about halfway to the village.[122]

Otto farm. *Author.*

The road toward Sharpsburg was in a deep valley, making it a dangerous avenue of attack. The buildings of the Otto and Sherrick farms gave additional cover to the defenders. John H. Stevenson of the 100th Pennsylvania, another new unit, recalled, "The regiment, after crossing, was sent out as skirmishers, and acted their part of the play as well as they knew how." Behind them, Colonel Thomas Welsh deployed the Forty-Fifth Pennsylvania on the right, the Forty-Sixth New York in the center and the Eighth Michigan on the left. George Crook's Ohio brigade was behind in support, a single brigade that would not have been enough to exploit any breakthrough.[123]

Marius King McDowell of the 100th Pennsylvania noted,

> [We] *went up a hill as skirmishers. When we reached the top of the hill the Confederate skirmish line began firing on us from behind a fence—we couldn't see them but we fired back at the fence as best we could.*
>
> *I had fired off my gun only once after reaching the hilltop and was on my knees reloading when I was shot in the right thigh by a…ball, which lodged in my leg. I finished reloading my gun and fired at a house which seemed to serve as a fort to the rebels* [the Otto House]. *The sergeant of*

Sherrick farm. *Library of Congress.*

> *my company, seeing I was wounded, ordered John Graham to take me back to the rear. John Graham could not do it alone so James McCreary helped him. One held me up on either side as I could use only one leg.*
>
> *When we reached Burnside's bridge again, they were going to take me over it but the rebels had gotten range of the bridge and were shelling it. Instead of attempting to go over it, we went under it, wading right into the water. The shelling was so heavy we stayed under the bridge until it seemed as if the bridge would be battered down. We waded out on the other side of the Antietam Creek—I dropped my gun into the river as I saw I would not need it again.*[124]

Fred Pettit, of the same unit, noted,

> *We advanced to the top of the first hill where we could see their riflemen firing from behind a stone wall at about 400 yards distant. There were two…batteries about 800 yards from us which piled shot, shell, and grape, and railroad iron at us thick and strong.*
>
> *We fired at the riflemen, and soon made them run. We then ran forwards about 100 yards to some grain stacks and commenced* [firing] *on their*

> *artillerymen, at about 700 yards. We soon made them leave with their guns. The other battery was out of sight so we could not get at it.*
>
> *I then became separated from my regiment but went forward some distance with other regiments, but not finding our regiment I came back again and found John Wilson wounded in the leg. I then helped him off towards the hospital.*[125]

Artillery support assisted the advance. Brigade commander Colonel Thomas Welsh wrote,

> *I moved my command over a steep hill, immediately charging the enemy and driving them rapidly in the direction of Sharpsburg, my troops advancing to the edge of the town and capturing the rebel Captain Twiggs and several soldiers.*
>
> *Discovering that we had advanced beyond our supporting forces on our right, and also on our left, I withdrew my command to an orchard directly on the left of Colonel Christ, Frist Brigade of the Division. We remained in this position until ordered back by the general commanding, to the support of the forces then desperately engaged with the enemy, who were endeavoring to outflank us on our left.*
>
> *My command was exposed for several hours to a tremendous cross-fire from the artillery of the enemy, as well as a direct fire from their infantry and riflemen in our front, yet they advanced with steadiness and rapidity, driving the enemy at all points and performing strictly the great duty devolved on them by the commanding general….I had great difficulty in restraining the ardor of my troops, who seemed anxious to charge through the town and capture the batteries beyond.*[126]

According to its monument, the 100th Pennsylvania advanced 495 yards west and north of the Ninth New York's prominent monument, on a ridge overlooking the southeast corner of Sharpsburg, perhaps 200 yards from the town. There they halted, encountering stiff resistance and having no support. Lieutenant Colonel Joseph Gerhardt of the Forty-Sixth New York described how after crossing the bridge, they ascended a steep hill on the left (south) side of the road and immediately were hit with "a galling fire of shot and shell."[127]

Welsh's men made it up to the edge of town on the road. They captured several Confederates who had held out at Lumm's imposing stone mill. The Federals continued advancing up the road toward the town. One veteran of

Area crossed by the 100th Pennsylvania, advancing left to right on the hill in the distance. *Author.*

the Forty-Fifth Pennsylvania wrote afterward that they "entered Sharpsburg" and "drove the rebels through the town," both clearly exaggerations. The advance likely reached High Street near the Avery House, but no Union troops entered the town in force.[128]

The halt of the Fifth Corps units on their right, combined with the stiffening Confederate resistance in their front and low ammunition, convinced Christ and Welsh to halt. The South Carolinians remained on the high ground overlooking Lumm's Mill, having slowed the timid Union advance enough to halt it. In the meantime to their right, Drayton's and Kemper's brigades were falling back in front of the advance of Welsh's brigade, so Colonel Joseph Walker ordered the brigade to retreat as well. They repositioned to be parallel with the ravine through which the road to town ran, facing south, and fired on the flank of the Forty-Fifth Pennsylvania. The brigade then changed again to face the east. No one knew it yet, but their work at Antietam was finished.[129]

While Jenkins's brigade was holding off Christ, General Thomas Drayton's South Carolina brigade took cover behind a stone wall at the

Lumm's Mill. *Author.*

edge of an orchard below the McCraw House, south of the road that ran into town from the bridge. The Fifteenth used the buildings for cover and prepared to make their stand there. Colonel Bradley T. Johnson noted that they were "holding on with desperate tenacity to the stone barn and houses." General David Jones noted that they were "slowly and in good order, forming the nucleus on which the brigade rallied." Led by Colonel William D. DeSaussure, the Fifteenth South Carolina had smoothbore .69 caliber muskets and were using buck and ball ammunition. These weapons were not as accurate as rifles, but with buck and ball (a large ball and two smaller ones), they could inflict maximum damage at close range. The Forty-Fifth Pennsylvania halted in a ravine under heavy fire, and here the Union advance stalled.[130]

The rest of Jones's division was on high ground behind a stone wall with a rail fence, where the Ninth New York monument now stands. From left to right, Drayton's units were the Fifteenth South Carolina, Fiftieth Georgia, and Phillips Legion (Georgia). Kemper's regiments were the Third South Carlina Battalion, Fifty-First Georgia, Eleventh Virginia, First Virginia, Seventh Virginia and Seventeenth Virginia. Private David E. Johnston of the Seventh Virgina noted that the regiments were all understrength: the whole brigade was at about 400 men, and the Seventh itself had only 113. Captain J.S. Brown's Wise Artillery (Virginia) assisted them here.[131]

To Drayton's right, General James Kemper sent the Twenty-Fourth and the Seventh Virginia to the south and right of his brigade, along the Harpers Ferry Road. The Twenty-Fourth halted in an open field east of the road, north of a strip of corn that ran toward the forty-acre cornfield. There, they were on the far right of the army. The Seventh took position at the southeast edge of the strip of corn. Kemper's understrength brigade had only about two hundred men in its four Virginia regiments. They were deployed with the Seventeenth on the right and the Seventh next in line. The Eleventh Virginia from the Lynchburg area had only eighty-five men, led by Captain Mitchell. The Seventeenth Virginia under Colonel Montgomery D. Corse, on the brigade's right, had only fifty-five men in line.[132]

Private John Dooley of the First Virginia stated that they were in front of the town in an orchard, some behind a stone wall and most behind a rail fence on the border of a cornfield. The entire regiment had only twenty-six men, but two guns nearby provided support.[133]

Opposing them were Welsh's four regiments, and off to Welsh's left, Colonel Harrison Fairchild was bringing up the Ninth, 103rd and Eighty-Ninth New York. And farther to Fairchild's left, Colonel Harland's strung-out brigade was slowly coming up. The Ninth New York advanced to within thirty yards of the Fifteenth South Carolina, and the two units traded volleys. Finally pulling back, the South Carolinians retreated to the west. Private Thomas Hare of the Eighty-Ninth New York seized their flag at the stone wall. It was an Army of Northern Virginia pattern wool bunting flag that they had received only two months earlier. Hare was killed later in the day but posthumously was awarded the Medal of Honor for the capture.[134]

After three o'clock in the afternoon, Union skirmishers appeared in front of the Seventh Virginia, in position behind a rail fence. The 103rd New York's main line followed five hundred yards behind the skirmishers. As the Federals advanced, Drayton and Kemper fell back two hundred yards to the Harpers Ferry Road. Here, they took position behind an old board fence and embankment, south of a strip of corn. The Seventh and Twenty-Fourth regiments occupied two hundred yards and were separated from the right of Kemper's line by about five hundred yards.[135]

Fearful of being hit in the back, John Dooley of the First Virginia occasionally turned around to avoid this disgraceful fate. In the distance behind him, he heard the Union troops cheer at the stone fence, as if they had won a "base ball" game. Breathless, he reached the edge of the cornfield, where Toombs's Georgians were rallying at the road, and the Virginians reformed alongside them. Dooley noted how Toombs rode up and down the line, inspiring his men with his words.[136]

The men of the First and Eleventh Virginia heard voices and drums from the Eighty-Ninth and 103rd New York in their front. Toombs's Georgians had fallen back to defend the Harpers Ferry Road with the Fifteenth, Seventeenth and Eleventh Georgia, and the Twentieth rejoined them with fresh ammunition. The Eleventh Georgia, 140 strong, had sent half of its men to bolster the Confederate left at seven thirty that morning; the remainder stayed with Toombs.[137]

Captain Ashby of the Seventh Virginia yelled to his troops, "Men, we are to hold this position at all hazards. Not a man leave his place. If need be, we will die together here in this road." They took cover behind a fence with a cornfield in front, the men placing their "muskets through the board fence, and with our fingers on the triggers." Jenkins, Kemper and Drayton were outnumbered and had no reserve.[138]

Several Union batteries had crossed the creek and deployed on the high ground west of it near Otto's Lane, including Durell, Clark and Muhlenberg. Their fire dismounted one gun of Garden's Palmetto battery and killed several horses. The surviving crew members hitched up the other gun and pulled out.

As the Union troops advanced to the nearest height, the First Virginia fired at the heads that emerged over the crest. The Eighty-Ninth and 103rd New York then charged up to their fence. Dooley recalled, "Hastily emptying our muskets into their lines, we fled back through the cornfield." He recalled it was hard to run through the corn with his rifle and gear, and he felt like he was moving at "half speed." Not wanting to be shot in the back, he also frequently turned around to run backward. Major Hebert and Lieutenant Thomas Perry of the Seventh Virginia were captured at the wall but able to escape later. Colonel Montgomery Corse was wounded in the foot and captured, turning down his uniform collar to hide rank. A Union solder pointed a pistol at him, but an officer intervened to protect him.[139]

Behind the fence at the road, Private David E. Johnston of the Seventh Virginia wrote that they "placed our guns through the board fence, drawn back the hammers, and stood with fingers on triggers, ready to fire as soon as the enemy emerged from the corn, with the eastern edge of which his lines has about reached."[140]

Alexander Hunter of the Seventeenth Virginia noted that artillery fire suddenly came in, and they prepared for the infantry to attack next. A shell

Otto Lane. Union troops sought shelter in this prominent landmark. *Author.*

hit Private Appich, tearing him apart and spraying his blood over the troops nearby. The men waited behind a fence with rifles resting on the lower rails. Behind them, officers cautioned, "Steady!" The outnumbered Confederates could hear the Union officers shouting as the enemy approached but could not yet see them.[141]

Hunter wrote vividly, "We saw the gilt eagles on the flag-poles emerge over the top of the hill, followed by the flags drooping on their staffs. Then the tops of the caps appeared, and next a line of the fiercest eyes men ever looked upon." The Confederates fired at sixty yards, and Hunter noted,

> *It staggered them—it was a murderous fire—and many fell; some of them struck for the rear, but the majority sent a stunning volley at us, and but for that fence there would have been hardly a man left alive. The rail, posts, were shattered by the balls; but still it was a deadly one—fully one half of the Seventeenth lay in their tracks; the balance that is left load and fire again and again and for about ten minutes the unequal struggle is kept up.*

Of the fifty-five men in the command, they lost thirty-one killed and ten captured: forty-one of fifty-five. The fence was "a thing of shreds and patches," Hunter noted after the battle.[142]

Hunter, who had only rejoined the Seventeenth Virginia after being captured and exchanged, noted that as they waited along the Harpers Ferry Road, the men became "cramped from lying in their constrained position; some were moving up and down, some stretching themselves."[143]

Alexander Hunter, facing the Eighty-Ninth and the 103rd New York, wrote,

> *All the guns went off at once, and the whole brigade fire seemed to follow our volley, and the enemy's line, sadly thinned, broke and went over the hill. Every man in our line began to load his musket with frenzied haste. Only three or four of the Seventeenth were shot, the fire of the enemy being too high.*
>
> *We had barely loaded and capped the muskets when the blue line came with a rush and we fired now without orders. Before we could load a third time the two lines of battle of the Federals, now commingled as one solid bank of men, poured a volley into us that settled the matter. It killed or wounded every officer and man in the regiment except five, of whom I was fortunate enough to be one.*
>
> *Just as the bluecoats were climbing the fence I threw down my musket and raised my hand in token of surrender. Two or three stopped to carry me back to the rear. The rest kept on, urged by their officers, in the direction of the village of Sharpsburg.*
>
> *Major Hebert and Lieutenant Perry made a dash for the rear and escaped. I and a private named Gunnell, of the Fairfax Rifles, were the only prisoners; the rest of the regiment lay there motionless in their positions. The men were either lying down or kneeling—the wounds were dangerous or deadly. But for the protection afforded by the fence I do not believe that a single man of the regiment would have escaped alive.*[144]

Confederate artillery was concentrating in the area to bolster the line and support the outnumbered infantry. Pegram's, Crenshaw's, Eshleman's, Elliott's, Boyce's, Carter's, Latham's, Manly's, Reilly's and Maurin's batteries all deployed southeast of Sharpsburg. Several modern histories discuss General James Longstreet and staff arriving to help serve on a battery here. Many of the Antietam battlefield guides assert that this took place near the Piper Farm instead.[145]

Major B.W. Frobel, chief of artillery in Reilly's battery, wrote: "I cannot too highly applaud the conduct of both officers and men. Captains Bachman and Reilly fought their batteries with their usual determination." Around two o'clock in the afternoon, the left section of Reilly's North Carolina battery, two howitzers, received fresh ammunition and took position on the hill behind Toombs's troops. Here they fired on the advancing Federals until Frobel ordered them to retire, having fired seventy-four rounds and with one gun disabled. With all of the battery's horses hit, the exhausted gunners moved the pieces off by hand.[146]

An hour later the right section's ten-pound Parrott guns, led by Lieutenant John Ramsay, received ammunition and moved forward to support the others. Ramsey met General Lee, and both saw troops advancing toward the Confederate flank. Lee asked what troops they were, and Ramsey handed him his binoculars. His hands bandaged from a recent accident, Lee said, "Can't use."

Looking himself, Ramsay said, "They are flying the United States flag."

Pointing to another group in the far distance, Lee asked, "What troops are those?"

Ramsey replied, "They are flying the Virginia and Confederate flags."

"It is A.P. Hill, from Harpers Ferry," noted Lee, and he ordered Ramsay to put his guns on a knoll beside the Harpers Ferry Road.[147]

While these actions unfolded, Lee was watching events closely, likely moving from the north to a position south and west of Sharpsburg. When General A.P. Hill arrived, Lee instructed him where to bring his division into the fray. Hill's troops likely marched straight north on farm lanes from Pack Horse Ford, as General William T. Pendleton had overseen the improvement of roads and river access. The division then turned right (east) until they struck Miller's Sawmill Road, which led them to the right spot to enter the battlefield. Either Hill or a staff officer or messenger then communicated with Jones, and word trickled down to the brigade and regimental commanders that Hill was on the way.[148]

Positioned at the center of the Union line was General Cox. Seeing the collapse of Rodman's division on the left and the check of the troops to his front (Fairchild's brigade), he realized that he had to reign in Willcox's advance. He ordered Willcox to retire and Sturgis's division to come forward from the reserve to bolster the line in place of Rodman's fleeing troops. This story is told in more detail in the next three chapters.[149]

Chapter 4

HIGH TIDE

The advance of Rodman's and Willcox's divisions occurred simultaneously, so it must be remembered that the events described here are broken down by area to cover them in detail. There were two high tides in the fields southeast of Sharpsburg: the advance and repulse of the Ninth, Eighty-Ninth and 103rd New York and that of the Eighth Connecticut. The New Yorkers crested first, followed shortly after by the New Englanders.

Arriving at about three o'clock in the afternoon from Pack Horse Ford in the lead of Hill's division, Captain David McIntosh unlimbered the Pee Dee (South Carolina) battery to the right and rear of Toombs's position, with Pegram's battery to their right. Hurried on by a staff officer, McIntosh deployed without one of his guns, it having broken down on the way. The battery's twenty-one exhausted men were not enough to adequately serve the three cannons. Officers and men, cannoneers and horse drivers all stepped in to work the pieces. Their horses, taken from Union batteries captured at Harpers Ferry, were worn out from the forced march.[150]

According to McIntosh, they

> *opened on a heavy column passing to the left across our front. As they came into full view, emerging from a ravine in front, we fired double charges of canister at short range, and with terrible effect. I directed the guns to be trained on the colors of the regiments, and more than once they were swept down with a huge gap in the ranks on either side.*

Map of troop positions at 4:20 p.m. *Hal Jespersen.*

The battery was to the left of Toombs's troops, with a cornfield on their right. With the Eighth Connecticut closing in and his guns low on ammunition, McIntosh gave the order to withdraw and leave the guns, writing, "We pulled off some of the limbers, and left the guns in the possession of the enemy, but in a short time they were retaken by Toombs' Brigade."[151]

Sixteen-year-old Baxter Rollins was a color-bearer with McIntosh's Battery. Seeing they were going to be overrun, Baxter planted the flag between the guns and jumped into the no. 4 position on a Napoleon. In this position, Baxter's role was to pull the lanyard that sets off the gun. While he was in the act of pulling the lanyard, a shell hit him in the side, wounding him, and he fell, the motion of his body firing the piece. The cannon's recoil caused a wheel to roll over and crush his foot. His comrades put him on a blanket to

McIntosh's Battery position. *Author.*

carry him off, but he protested, saying, "Don't carry me to the rear, boys, I know I've got to die—carry me to my flag, I must die by my flag." Rollins was captured and died of his wounds in Union hands.[152]

McIntosh's battery lost most of its newly captured horses in the fray. Seeing the crisis unfolding, Captain William J. Pegram directed his Purcell battery (Virginia) to fire on the flank of the attacking New Englanders. Pegram was later wounded.[153]

While General Orlando B. Willcox's division advanced toward Sharpsburg on the Ninth Corps' right, General Isaac P. Rodman's division began moving west toward the Harpers Ferry Road. Rodman ordered Harland and Fairchild forward, and Harland passed the message on to his units. The 421 men of the Eighth Connecticut moved out, climbing the rising ground toward the Harpers Ferry Road. Tragically, the other two units, the Fourth Rhode Island and the Sixteenth Connecticut, did not hear the order and remained behind in a forty-acre cornfield in the low ground below Otto's Lane. In the meantime, the Eighth Connecticut was far out ahead of the rest of the regiments in Harland's brigade. The advance of Rodman's force was very disjointed, with Fairchild's brigade moving out in front and Harland's lagging behind on the left. Behind them was Ewing's brigade with Colonel Scammon, who was virtually reduced to an observer, his two brigades split up to support Willcox and Rodman.[154]

Private David E. Johnston of the Seventh Virginia recalled that when Fairchild and Harland advanced, their skirmishers were in front at a rail fence at the base of the hill (modern Branch Avenue). The Seventh and Twenty-Fourth Virginia then fell back to the Harpers Ferry Road, behind an old board fence and embankment just south of the narrow strip of corn. He estimated that there were about two hundred yards between the Seventh and the Twenty-Fourth and about four or five hundred yards between the Seventh and Seventeenth Virginia of Kemper's brigade. Here they faced the Eighty-Ninth New York. A soldier in the Fifteenth Georgia recalled using a rail fence for cover and firing with their "trusty Enfield's."[155]

Lieutenant Graham of the Ninth New York recalled vividly,

> *I turned over quickly to look at Colonel Kimball, who had given the order, thinking he had become suddenly insane, never dreaming that he intended to advance in that fire, and firmly believing that the regiment would not last one minute after the men had got fairly on their feet. Sure enough, there was Kimball....He repeated the order: "Get up Ninth!"*[156]

The men eagerly sprang to their feet; the anticipation and suspense of waiting while under fire was taxing. At the top of the hill, they were exposed to artillery fire but could not see the enemy. Moving west over fences and down into a valley, they lost men all the way. They began to ascend another hill. J.E. Whitney wrote that "fences and other obstructions had to be surmounted, and many fell in the various attitudes of climbing."

Cresting this second hill, they were met with a "tornado of shot and shell" from a battery on their right, which enfiladed them. Along the way, they yelled out their unique battle cry of "Zoo-zoo-zoo." Gaining the crest, they halted to catch their breath. Colonel Edgar Kimball ordered the regiment's bugler to play "Assembly of the Ninth." Heard above the noise of battle, the tune rallied the men, guided stragglers and was an act of defiance to enemy in front. Behind them, their path was strewn with killed and wounded.

When the New Yorkers of Fairchild's brigade stepped off from the relative shelter of Otto's Lane, they immediately entered the beaten (impact) zone. They had been within artillery range the entire time since fording the creek, and now as they climbed over the fence along the lane and moved into the ravine below, they came into rifle range. From left to right, the Eighty-Ninth

Harland's brigade's view of the final attack. The New Yorkers charged over the rising ground to the distant ridge. *Author.*

New York, the 103rd New York and the colorful Ninth New York moved toward the Confederate line along the stone wall at the crest of a ridge, about 450 yards away. Only Drayton's and Kemper's small brigades were in front of them, but A.P. Hill's advanced units under Gregg and Branch were about to hit Harland's scattered units to the south. Despite outnumbering the enemy, the Union advance lacked enough support to exploit a breakthrough (only Sturgis's division, which had fought in the morning, was in reserve).

One soldier had his lower jaw shot off yet waved his fez to inspire his comrades. Seeing this, Kimball shouted, "See that? Isn't *that* enough to make you fight?" The Ninth New York advanced again, now taking rifle fire and having lost about two hundred men. The wall ahead of them bristled with the muskets of Drayton's troops. The New Yorkers had held their fire till now but began to earnestly return fire when about fifty yards away. Rushing up to the wall, they mounted it as the Confederates fell back. A few who remained were taken prisoner.

Color Sergeant Myers was hit and fell but held the Ninth's flag up as he lay on the ground until another took it from him, but this man was then hit.

A third man took it up but was also soon struck. A young solider then took the flag and ran out in front of the line, was hit and fell. Two more then took up the flag; each were hit. A total of eight men were killed or wounded carrying the regiment's flag that day.[157]

When the Ninth's color guard went down, Captain Adolphe Libaire, a "quiet, modest" and "unassuming" French recruit, jumped up and grabbed the regimental flag, yelling, "Up damn you, and forward!" For his actions, Libaire earned the Medal of Honor, his citation stating, "In the advance on the enemy and after his color bearer and the entire color guard of eight men had been shot down, this officer seized the regimental flag and with conspicuous gallantry carried it to the extreme front, urging the line forward."[158]

The Ninth New York of Fairchild's brigade carried both a national flag and a unique six-by-eight-foot red silk battle flag with the golden inscription "9th Regiment, N.Y.V., Toujours Prêt" on the center, French for "Always Ready." The regiment had 373 men. Edward K. Wightman of Ninth New York wrote a few days later,

> *In common with the other two regiments of Hawkins Brigade (the 89th and 103rd New York) they assaulted a battery posted on a hill and defended by a whole division of the enemy. The boys charged gallantly over two ridges of ploughed land up to the mouths of the guns, but their ammunition failing there, and getting no support from a second brigade, appointed to act in concert with them, they were forced to fall back after holding their newly taken position fifteen minutes in the face of a withering fire. Our color guards were cut down almost to a man, and Kimball, our hot headed Lieut. Colonel, finally sized the flag himself and wrapped it round him. Strange to say, he was uninjured.*[159]

The Ninth New York's regimental flagstaff had a silver plate inscribed with: "Presented by Mrs. Adelaide W. Griswold to the Ninth Regiment New York Volunteers. June 5th, 1861. Lexington, April Nineteenth, 1776. Baltimore, April Nineteenth, 1861. Memoria in Eterna." The references to Lexington and the early war riot in Baltimore were clear patriotic symbols on their flagstaff.[160]

As the Eighty-Ninth New York approached the stone wall, Sergeant Stacey A. Stearns tackled a tall Confederate who refused to surrender. The Confederate was drawing a knife when Stearns stabbed him with his bayonet. When his comrades asked why he didn't try to take him prisoner, the sergeant said, "The terms were not satisfactory." Yet many were taken as

Sketch by David Thomas of the Ninth New York, showing the attack. *Ninth New York Regimental File, Antietam National Battlefield.*

the Confederates fell back. Some of the prisoners they captured were from the Third Georgia, whom the unit had encountered on the North Carolina coast earlier that year at the battle of South Mills.[161]

The ravine to the west of Otto Lane offered a bit of shelter, but as the Union forces ascended and closed in on the Confederates, they came within view again of Kemper's and Drayton's men, about 450 yards away. As the New Yorkers advanced, they took increasing rifle fire, and the right unit, the Ninth, had no shelter. A slight ravine offered some cover for the Eighty-Ninth, on the left. A Zouave in the Ninth regiment wrote of going down into the hollow in front of them and ascending the next hill under "terrible fire." Then,

> *The order came for us to go forward which we did on a double quick as we came to the brow of hill and over it a terrible fire was concentrated upon our little band but on we pushed....Bullets came in terrible showers and from all sides of us.*[162]

The ground was open, and the Confederates were ready. Rodman's troops had to move over half a mile of open, rolling ground, where three

Confederate batteries of artillery could converge their fire on the area (Reilly, Brown and Richardson). "The prospect was far from encouraging but the order came to get ready for the attempt," said David Thompson of the Ninth New York.[163]

Corporal Burton Hine of the Eighty-Ninth New York described the attack:

> *Our company was ordered to go forward and skirmish which we did and drove back the rebel skirmishers. Our Brigade was ordered forward on a charge. The fight was on, and the men fell on both sides, and first knew, the rebels had flanked us and then all was confusion, every man doing the best he could.*

Hine got separated from his men and ended up fighting with some of the Eighth Connecticut (which was advancing to the left of his unit). "The rebels cut them down," he recalled, "and we were obliged to fall back.[164]

Charles Johnson of the Ninth New York wrote of how they advanced to the hilltop with artillery plowing up the earth around them, shells bouncing into and around the men. His company advanced in front as skirmishers, up over the crest and to a fence. Then, he noted, "We could see, at a distance of about six hundred yards, a body of skirmishers playing away behind a stone wall, while on a hill behind them was the main body." Here they lay down and returned fire.[165]

The Thirty-Fifth Massachusetts had advanced to Otto Lane, where they could see but remained in reserve. From a half mile away in the rear, the Bay State troops watched the charge of the Ninth New York go forward toward the Harpers Ferry Road. An observer wrote, "It was a pretty sight.... It began to look like victory."[166]

Private David Thompson of the Ninth New York wrote of the chaos of battle,

> *It is astonishing how soon, and by what slight causes, regularity of formation and movement are lost in actual battle. Disintegration begins with the first shot. To the book-soldier all order seems destroyed, months of drill apparently going for nothing in a few minutes. Next after the most powerful factor in this derangement—the enemy—come natural obstacles and the inequalities of the ground.*
>
> *Our knapsacks were left on the ground behind us. At the word a rush was made for the fences. The line was so disordered by the time the second fence was passed that we hurried forward to a shallow undulation a few feet*

> *ahead, and lay down among the furrows to re-form, doing so by crawling up into line. A hundred feet or so ahead was a similar undulation to which we ran for a second shelter.*
>
> *As the range grew better, the firing became more rapid, the situation desperate and exasperating to the last degree. Human nature was on the rack, and there burst forth from it the most vehement, terrible swearing I have ever heard.*

They rose up and charged again, wounded men falling all around. Thompson wrote, "The mental strain was so great that I saw at that moment the singular effect mentioned, I think, in the life of Goethe on a similar occasion, the whole landscape for an instant turned slightly red." He then stated a feeling probably shared by many soldiers that day:

> *The truth is, when bullets are whacking against tree-trunks and solid shot are cracking skulls like egg-shells, the consuming passion in the breast of the average man is to get out of the way. Between the physical fear of going forward, and the moral fear of turning back, there is a predicament of exceptional awkwardness from which a hidden hole in the ground would be a wonderfully welcome outlet.*[167]

Lieutenant Matthew J. Graham of the Ninth New York detailed the action:

> *I was lying on my back, supported on my elbows, watching the shells explode overhead, and speculating as to how long I could hold up my finger before it would be shot off, for the very air seemed full of bullets, when the order to get up was given.… We got up and went forward, passing at once into a cornfield. The fence over which my men were swarming was at that moment knocked down by a shell. From the corn we crossed over a meadow, then over a stirp of plowed land, and then another piece of grass. We halted twice, I think, to rest and dress the line.… The loss was frightful. I could see the regiment…shortening perceptibly as we advanced.*
>
> *The charge ended, so far as I was concerned, in what appeared to be a grand finale. We had been advancing over what I remembered as rolling, but at the same time rising ground; we had reached what looked like the summit of this particular ridge, when we were met by what I remember as a crashing volley of musketry. We all went down together, although I was hit not with a bullet, but with a grapeshot. The fronts of the companies had by that time become so narrow that I found myself right at the colors. The*

> *companies did not average, I think, above twelve or fifteen men each, at that stage. When I recovered myself after I fell—that is, got into position to see about me, and after the men had passed over me, some stumbling over and others stepping on me…nearly everybody was down on the ground. The whole color guard lay prone, the colors on the ground. One or two of the men staggered to their feet and reached for the colors, but were shot down at once. Then there was what seemed a spontaneous rush for them by a dozen or more men…who were shot down in succession as each one raised his flag. The flags were up and down, up and down, several times in a minute. Lebaier at once seized one of them, and swinging it around his head was profane for the first and only time, I think, shouting to his company, "Up damn you, and forward!" I could see only toward the right to the line as I lay. Kimball, Horner, Lebaier and McKechnie, all shouting forward as the men sprang to their feet. McKechnie was on the stone wall with his fez on the point of his sword waving his men on.*[168]

Lieutenant Colonel Edgar Kimball wrote in his report,

> *We proceeding by the right flank along the bluff of the creek for about three-fourths of a mile to the brow of a hill, till within about eight hundred yards of the enemy's main body of artillery and infantry. Here we halted for rest, when the rebels opened an unmerciful fire of shot and shell upon us, killing and wounding a number of my regiment, and shooting my horse from under me by the explosion of a shrapnel.*
>
> *We were soon ordered to advance, which was promptly done, the different battalions moving in line of battle, and dressing on their colors, with as much coolness and accuracy as though upon the drill ground instead of the battle field. After proceeding about two hundred yards you ordered the charge to be made, when we rushed forward with a wild huzzah, peculiar, to the Zouaves, and immediately received the fire of thousands of the enemy's fresh troops, consisting of artillery and infantry, which had been brought forward to meet us. At this time the gallant Cooper fell. A shell fell in my lines, killing eight men at one explosion; a round shot took off private Conway's head. While the infantry fire was like hail around and among us, producing the most dreadful carnage, not a man who was not wounded wavered or faltered, but all pressed on with charged bayonets to the top of the hill and drove the enemy from his position.*
>
> *At this time our color-bearers and guard had all been shot down, when Capt. Lebair, of company F, seized one, and Capt. Leahy, of company I,*

> *the other of our standards, and advanced them to the wall near the road, when the rout of the enemy at this point, became complete. After crossing the road and ravine the enemy promptly rallied and attempted to turn upon us by a flank movement on our left, but were prevented by the Eighty-ninth, under command of Major Jardine of the Ninth, who gave them the bayonet, and captured their colors, which proved to be those of a South Carolina regiment, and completing the victory at this point.*
>
> *After resting here for a short time, and finding the enemy massing fresh troops in large force, on our left, we were ordered to retire and take position about four hundred yards in the rear of the one we then occupied, which change was executed in good order and without confusion. After remaining in this position for a short time we were positively ordered to withdraw from the greater part of the field we had won. The men retired in good order, at a slow step, and with tears in their eyes, at the necessity which compelled them to leave the field they had so dearly won, and bivouacked for the night. Thus ended one of the hardest battles ever fought on this continent.*[169]

Private Charles F. Johnson of the same unit also noted the incoming ordnance: "Nothing less than stumps of railroad iron as long as my arm. If this was not adding insult to injury! But we could pay little attention to these unwelcome missiles, and proceeded."[170]

Lieutenant Matthew Graham of the Ninth wrote, "All this took place in a flash, as it seems to me now." Unfortunately, Graham was hit in the leg and carried to the rear. He had given a detailed description of the Ninth New York's advance up to this point, and his continued observations would have been of immense benefit to historians. Taken to a field hospital, he was unable to observe any more of the action, and his detailed writings stop at this point.

Kimball reported that they charged with bayonets fixed as shells fell thickly among them like hail, one killing eight at once. The color guard were all shot down, and Captain Libaire sized one flag and Captain Leahy the other. They advanced with the flags to the wall at the road." Despite Graham's claim, the Federals did not reach the Harpers Ferry Road.[171]

Colonel Harrison S. Fairchild recalled that his brigade charged to a fence that the Confederates had abandoned. In need of support, he requested the other brigade (Harland's). Yet Harland was having his own issues as Gregg's attack sliced into his scattered units (see chapter 6). Fairchild's troops remained "at this position" in front and exposed until ordered back, and he noted that officers and men regretted the withdrawal.[172]

The charge of the Ninth New York. *Battles and Leaders.*

Private Johnson saw it clearly: "At a distance of about six hundred yards, a body of skirmishers playing away behind a stone wall, while on a hill behind them was the main body." This refers to the Confederate skirmishers at the stone wall and the main line on the Harpers Ferry Road behind them. "I had fired about a dozen rounds," wrote Johnston, "when I found that some of my cartridges were useless, those in the bottom of the box having become wet while we were crossing the stream." He also described the advance as done with "wild speed."

At the stone wall abandoned by the Confederates, Johnson recorded, "I was in a delirium, I was mad," due to the loss of his comrades. He continued, "The air was filled with a deluge of bullets, grape, canister and shell….I saw the Rebels quite plainly through the smoke and dust of the cornfield, going through the motions of firing and loading." Johnson stood there "with nothing left in my cartridge box" and one shot loaded in his rifle. Finding himself isolated and alone, amid incoming fire, he wrote, "I became pretty much excited."[173]

By now, the Eighty-Ninth and the 103rd New York had fallen back, leaving the Ninth alone and isolated. Major L.C. Brackett of General Willcox's staff arrived and told Kimball to fall back, but the New Yorker objected. Brackett realized he couldn't compel him, as Kimball and the Ninth New York were in Rodman's division, not Willcox's. Kimball believed help was on the way and didn't want to stop their advance. Then General Willcox rode up and ordered Kimball to fix bayonets and fall back. The Zouaves were low on ammunition and could see the Confederates gathering for an advance. Lieutenant Matthew Graham stated that they fell back "in good order," but he may have been putting things in the best light.

Private David L. Stage of the Ninth had just returned from recovering at a hospital and was told to not to go into battle this day. Insisting he would, Stage was wounded five times in the action and left on the battlefield that night. He lay two days without food and water before his comrades reached him.

The Zouaves halted, and officers tried to reform their men and restore order, but under the circumstances, it was impossible. Men were scattered from the charge, the incoming fire was intense and adrenaline was flowing through their veins. Sergeant Peter Searing was far out in front and had to be brought back to the line by threats from Lieutenant Horner, wielding a revolver.[174]

Private Johnson looked over and saw Major Jardine leading the Eighty-Ninth New York with a captured Confederate flag in his hand. "His face was

The Ninth New York's monument stands at the site of the stone wall, where their charge crested. *Author.*

as calm and his manner as cool as though he was going through the ceremony on Parade, while, could the death messengers have left their shadows, as they flitted through the air, they could have clouded the sun."

Seeing the United States flag among the troops ahead of them, some of the New Yorkers thought it was a "trick." In fact, Jardine shouted, "For God's sake, don't fire on your own men!" Yet he had scarcely spoken when he saw his mistake, and in a louder voice, he yelled at them, "Boys, they are under false colors! Give them Hell!" Either the Seventeenth Virginia, facing the Eighty-Ninth New York, had a national flag, or the observers were mistaken. No other accounts mention Kemper's troops having a national flag, only troops in A.P. Hill's division, so this is one discrepancy that cannot be resolved.[175]

A lingering issue that veterans disagreed on after the battle is whether Union troops actually entered Sharpsburg. Postwar Union accounts mention reaching the buildings at the edge of town, but no Confederate accounts mention federal troops entering Sharpsburg, though there is a mention of a dead Zouave found in a village street. Willcox says they got into town, but his reporting might be wishful thinking. Cox said they got to the edge of town. Perhaps a handful of soldiers made it to some of the outer buildings of the village's southeast corner, but no organized unit made it into Sharpsburg.[176]

With their momentum stymied, the New Yorkers fell back, and Drayton and Kemper's brigades charged and retook the stone wall, losing few men in their counterattack. Lieutenant William W. Athey of the Seventeenth Virginia captured a blue silk guidon from the 103rd New York during the advance, which they somehow were able to recapture. Toombs's, Archer's and Branch's brigades all joined in this effort, explained in more detail later.[177]

Private Almon Reed wrote to his parents that the Confederate force on their left (the newly arrived Seventh and Thirty-Seventh North Carolina) compelled them to fall back. Hit in the right leg, Reed fell and lay still in the "disputed ground in the cross fire. Sometimes the Rebels were running over me, and sometimes our men. Finally, however, we were overpowered, and our forces driven from the field."[178]

Colonel Montgomery Corse, captured during the Union advance, was freed by Toombs's men as they swept forward. Corse had managed to hide his rank, and after the battle, General Lee promoted him to brigadier general for his actions.[179]

Corporal Burton Hine of the Eighty-Ninth New York wrote that after falling back, they "sat down tired out. Our color bearers were both shot dead." As the Ninth New York fell back, Colonel Edward Ferrero advanced the rookie Thirty-Fifth Massachusetts forward to stabilize the situation. They rested their rifles on the rail fence along Otto's Lane and began firing toward the Thirty-Third and Thirty-Seventh North Carolina of Branch's newly arrived brigade. They then clambered over the fence and advanced into the ravine to stop and collect the disorganized Zouaves.[180]

In the ravine, they could see Branch's and Toombs's troops of Hill's division ahead of them at the stone wall vacated by Ewing's Ohioans and the forty-acre cornfield to their left, which sheltered Gregg's South Carolinians. The New Englanders loaded and fired to the front and left, as Captain Tracy P. Cheever moved behind the men, encouraging them, "Pop away! Boys, pop away!"[181]

The unit's regimental history recorded a description of their position and the landscape in such detail that it is possible to stand in the same spot and envision their view:

> *Behind us was the slope of the hill down which we had come; in front was a ploughed field, sloping up to a wall of the most solid construction; about two hundred yards off; on the left front, cornfields with the high stalks and waving blades uncut. Behind these the hill rose more steeply to the summit, upon which were the enemy's batteries. Behind the wall and in the cornfield was the Confederate infantry: their right overlapping our left, making a cross fire upon our left companies.*[182]

Alexander Hunter of the Seventeenth Virginia had been captured by the New Yorkers and taken to the rear, but he and his guards stopped to watch the Union advance. Hunter wrote,

> *We, Yank and Reb, were sitting down taking a sociable smoke when all at once we were startled as if touched by an electric shock. The air was filled with bursting shells, as if a dozen batteries had opened at once from the direction of Sharpsburg, and while we stood gazing we saw emerging from a cornfield a long line of gray, musket barrels scintillating in the rays of the declining sun and the Southern battle flags gleaming redly against the dark background.*[183]

A Bay State soldier described the intensity of the combat: "It was work in dead earnest and intensely exciting. One spoke to his comrade, turned aside and, looking back, saw him weltering upon the ground; but there was no time for thought then—load and fire!—load and fire!" Rifles became too hot to hold and clogged from fouling, making it harder to ram. Low on ammunition, soldiers picked up cartridges from the dead and wounded around them. Officers also roamed behind the line, gathering cartridges from the dead and wounded. Captain William S. King was hit seven times during the fray.[184]

Two members of the Thirty-Fifth earned the Medal of Honor this afternoon. Nineteen-year-old Sergeant Marcus H. Haskell was hit but managed to help a wounded comrade off the field, and Private Frank M. Whitman received the award for "extraordinary heroism" as he was among the last to leave and saved the lives of several others.

As Fairchild's New Yorkers fell back, the Eighth Connecticut, the lead regiment of Harland's brigade, was moving up. Their attack brought them up a ravine, offering some shelter, and they emerged just south of where the New Yorkers had been. The two left companies of the Eighth Connecticut veered off to capture McIntosh's (South Carolina) battery on the right of the Seventeenth Virginia. The Eighth's monument stands about three hundred yards northeast of their most advanced position, according to the veterans (the monument was placed where land could be purchased).

A soldier in the Fiftieth Georgia wrote of seeing the abandonment of McIntosh's guns:

> *I shall never forget the scene that met my gaze as we reached the top of the hill. There stood the four guns naked and desolate, no living soul about them, no caissons or gunners; the ground lay strewed with dead horses and men. The gunners, who had worked their pieces until the enemy were within fifty yards of them…had given way, implored us as we charged past them to save their battery.*

The badly wounded Baxter Rollins was captured by the Eighth Connecticut and taken back to a field hospital in the rear but did not survive.[185]

The Eighth Connecticut then began receiving fire from the Seventh and Thirty-Seventh North Carolina, led by General Branch, as well as from McIntosh's (Pee Dee) battery. Private Samuel Jay Nettleton wrote that they moved straight up the ridge and received grape and canister from the guns. Henry Hall of the Eighth noted,

> *When we were in the field next to the one that contained the rebel batteries we stopped for a moment to breathe and then started on again with only one fence and a few rods of uneven ground between us and victory. As we rose*

> *the Hill to the fence, a terrible burst of every description of missile from the Battery was showered upon us.*[186]

Company K was on the very left flank of the Eighth and approached closest to McIntosh's guns. Led by Captain Charles L. Upham, they approached the abandoned cannons. Private Roger Ford wrote,

> *We got to the top of the hill or most of the top there was a man came & told Major Lyon* [Lion] *that there was a battery of 3 guns on the hill abandoned. My comp*[any] *was then detached to take the battery we started with a cheer we got within 6 or 7 rods* [about thirty-five yards] *of the battery when we saw the Rebs were lying down behind their guns. We opened on them before they had time to open on us....*
>
> *We played on them until we heard a yelling on our left & there came up a Rebel Brigade. We then commenced on them we were firing brisk when we heard them about we were surrounded on three sides. Still the men fought bravely. The Captain finally ordered us back to the Regt. they had been deployed into line. They were cutting us right & left & also in the front but with all to discourage* [us]....*The men fought like Tigers we started for the Regt & all the while the men were falling around me....The Regt was being cut bad as we were.*[187]

Colonel Henry L. Benning with the Georgians who had defended the bridge and then fallen back to the Harpers Ferry Road was ordered by General Toombs to move north and assist in stabilizing the line. Twice Toombs sent orders for Benning to move faster as they trudged north up the road. It was reported that the enemy had entered Sharpsburg. Moving past a field of corn, Benning saw the Union troops with the captured guns, and their line extended down to the road leading to the bridge. By now, it was known that A.P. Hill was on the way, for Toombs told Benning to hold the line until he arrived.

Using the corn for shelter, Colonel Henry Benning had the Eleventh, Fifteenth and Seventeenth Georgia fire into the Union troops. The Georgians were disorganized and intermingled but fired with enthusiasm. The Union defenders replied, but both sides were ineffective; Benning said it was "spirited but not effective—they shooting over us, we under them." In about ten minutes, the Union troops wavered and fell back. The Georgians then advanced and recovered the abandoned guns of McIntosh's battery. "Never was anything better managed," wrote Benning.[188]

The Eighth Connecticut's view of McIntosh's Battery postion, with the Harper's Ferry Road in the distance. *Author.*

Captain Charles Upham of the Eighth Connecticut recalled the arrival of the Confederates: "They came up company or division front and deployed on reaching the fence at the edge of the field. each division opening fire as soon as it came into line. We fell back to our regiment which changed front and engaged them."

Private Samuel Jay Nettleton wrote that they were

> *exposed to grape & canister we moved rapidly to the top* [of the ridge] *& were met with a volley from a Brigade behind a board fence 100 yards ahead. We used our muskets as well as possible & dropt down & loaded & fired 5 or 10 minutes when we were ordered to retire.*

The men of the Eighth Connecticut were isolated and alone, receiving fire from three directions. Sergeant Henry Hall wrote that he

> *lay down behind the dead body of a rebel and looked over his back to see the proceedings. A cannon ball drove me away from there just as Lt. Col.*

> *Appleman was wounded and then I was all around after that, doing all I could to encourage them and keep them steady.*

Captain Charles Coit noted,

> *For quite a time the bullets took us on three sides + it was evident to all that we could not hold our own but not a man stirred expected to load + fire + fall wounded. It was very affecting to have the men as they fell wounded turn to me as they did + say "Capt I have got it" or "Capt what shall I do I am wounded," I think hardly a man left the ranks of my Co. when wounded without asking permission in some way.*[189]

If any of them looked over their left shoulder for the rest of their brigade (Sixteenth Connecticut and Fourth Rhode Island), they would do so in vain. Captain Wolcott Marsh wrote,

> *We now returned their fire & the men went to their work as cooly as if on drill. But we were trapped on our left flank was a large corn field & it was full of rebels on our right was a high hill where they were pouring in a gauling* [fire] *Upon us & all this beside those in our front. Where was our support. Where was the first brigade none of them to be seen on the right where they had gone. Where was the 16th and 4th who were on our left....*
>
> *Alas! They had been repulsed. It was death to remain in this advanced position longer. The Lt. Colonel* [Appleman] *was wounded & taken to the rear....Capt Hoyt's company was as bad off on right they were suffering terribly but not a man faltered a steady & continual fire was returned against 7 times our more of our numbers but a few minutes had gone & it seemed as if the regit. must be entirely annihilated.*
>
> *The Major* [Ward] *seeing that it was more than folly to remain ordered us to fall back. But many of the men seemed determined no to leave & would yell you to each other "Boys Lets Never Retreat. No Never. The major yelled at the top of his voice in a pleading tone "Boys will you follow your colors Rally around them & follow me The word "Colors brought the men to their senses & the devoted little band rallied around them down the hill we continually facing about & firing."*[190]

First Lieutenant Roger M. Ford of Company K of the Eighth Connecticut, who had tried to capture McIntosh's guns, wrote,

> *We joined the Regt. the order was to change front to rear on first company which was done in good order. We then gave it to them again we gave as well as they gave but our position as terrible. We now had orders to fall back we done so but we halted & formed & commenced on them gave them lead & we sent some of them to their homes. we were ordered to move back again we done so & rallied the third time & the men were as fast for fighting as they were at first. We had about half of the men that went into the fight.*[191]

Horace Williams of the Eighth noted that they charged and did not halt until they reached the high ground and took two guns. Yet they had to abandon them and fall back, with over half of Company A lost. Soldier Horace Williams wrote that indeed they captured two cannons but had to abandon them. He noted, in a postwar article, "It was the hottest fight I ever saw." An Italian-born soldier was captured yet managed to get a weapon and took his two captors prisoner. Sergeant Willcox was shot in the face but kept fighting until he was hit and killed.[192]

In the meantime, General Isaac Rodman saw that Colonel Edward Harland's other two units, the Sixteenth Connecticut and the Fourth Rhode Island, were not keeping up, The two officers consulted just behind the advancing Eighth Connecticut. Harland asked if he should go bring up the wayward regiments, and Rodman replied that he would do so. As they talked, they could discern troops moving to their vulnerable left flank: A.P. Hill's division. From this viewpoint, they would have had a limited line of sight to the south but could catch glimpses of troops and see clouds of dust.

Harland recalled, "I turned…and saw some infantry belonging to the enemy advancing upon our left flank….If that were not checked it would be impossible to hold this part of the field." From his vantage point on the high ground with the Eighth Connecticut, General Rodman saw Gregg's flank attack coming and ordered the Fourth Rhode Island and the Sixteenth Connecticut to swing to left to face them, but he was hit before being able to put the order into action. The marker noting Rodman's death on the battlefield indicates that he was killed 265 yards to the south, placing him behind the Eighth Connecticut's advance.[193]

Rodman was hit by a ball in the lung, a painful wound, and fell from his horse. Two men from Company K of the Eighth, Seth D. Bingham and Timothy E. Hawley, heard Rodman's cries for help as they were falling back from the attack on McIntosh's battery. They carried the wounded general to a sheltered spot and, later, to the Rohrbach house, where he died a few days later. Of course he filed no report, and apparently no one interviewed the

Monument for the Eighth Connecticut. *Author.*

dying general, so we have no account from him of his division's movements or his intentions and impressions that afternoon, a serious gap in our understanding of crucial events. His aide Robert H. Ives was also mortally wounded at about the same time and also could not provide an account. Rodman going down here was a huge loss at a critical time.[194]

First Lieutenant Henry C. Hall of the Eighth Connecticut wrote,

> *The rebels soon saw our situation and commenced a move to flank us and take us Prisoners before our support could reach us. Just then Col* [A]*ppleman fell....The red flag of the rebs was now coming steadily upon us from three sides and in a few moments the open space between us and our friends would have been filled with foes, while our Major gave the command to retreat. But not until the order had been three times repeated did our gallant fellows obey, so busy were they with their fighting. Meanwhile the gallant Zouaves were doing nothing safely sheltered behind a protecting hill.*[195]

General Maxcey Gregg's brigade led A.P. Hill's division onto the field, followed by those of General Lawence O'Brien Branch and James Archer. Branch's North Carolinians advanced east from the Harpers Ferry Road and then swung north to hit the Eighth Connecticut in the flank. As with Gregg's brigade, these troops arrived at an opportune moment to inflict maximum damage on an unsuspecting enemy. Archer's brigade had less than 350 men, and many had replaced their old inferior muskets with superior Enfield and Springfield rifles at Harpers Ferry.[196]

The Eighteenth North Carolina

> *crossed the ridge to the left of the stacks and as we descended into the valley beyond, we saw the thin gray line retreated from a wooded ridge some 300 yards over the corn, into a valley that extended toward the town, with Burnside's victorious blue coats in vigorous pursuit. The lines met in this corn-covered valley, and the conflict was terrific, decisive. Burnside was hurled back and a route prevented.*[197]

The Seventh North Carolina advanced into a cornfield along the Harpers Ferry Road, followed by the Thirty-Seventh North Carolina; behind them were the Thirty-Third and Eighteenth regiments. The left of the Seventh was briefly undone by artillery fire; Private James Harris noted that "a cannon shot, or two, sped across the brow of the hill." The two Tar Heel units hit the Eighth Connecticut in the flank and rear, and the devastating fire caused them to fall back.[198]

Officers in the Thirty-Seventh North Carolina of Branch's brigade noted that the Eighth fell back in good order, reporting that they "held ground quite stubbornly, fought splendidly, and went off very deliberately, firing back at the Thirty-Seventh and waving its flag." A soldier in the Fiftieth Georgia tells it somewhat differently, as he recalled how they fired into the New Englanders, "volley after volley, until, utterly unable to face such terrible punishment, their whole line broke."[199]

As the New Englanders fell back, the troops of Toombs and Archer charged from the front, while Branch's newly arriving units charged from the south. After their successful charge, J.W. Lokey of the Twentieth Georgia noted that he had fired all forty of his cartridges in the attack. On the way back to get more ammunition, he picked up two Union haversacks, and that evening, he feasted on bacon, hardtack, coffee and sugar. Colonel William T. Millican of the Fifteenth Georgia fell mortally wounded and was captured during the counterattack while facing the Thirty-Fifth Massachusetts.[200]

As one of the North Carolina regiments passed J.W. Lokey of the Twentieth Georgia, he saw a color-bearer struck and go down. The men of that unit failed to notice, so Lokey ran over and picked up the flag, crying, "For God's sake men, take your colors with you!"[201]

Amid the Seventh North Carolina,

The Harpers Ferry Road was the Confederate last line of defense. Here Toombs's men took shelter and launched a counerattack against the Union troops in the distance. General Branch's North Carolinans advanced into the area from the right. *Author.*

> *A shell was exploded in its ranks with destructive effect and some confusion ensued. Company commanders at once exerted themselves to prevent further disorder and First Sergeant Thomas P. Mallory…who had borne the colors with conspicuous courage throughout the campaign, placed himself in front and appealed to the men to align themselves on the colors which they did under fire, then moving forward, the regiment occupied the stone wall.*[202]

Major William G. Morris, commanding the Thirty-Seventh North Carolina, stated that they went over a stone wall into a cornfield, received a "warm fire" and fell back to the wall. Then they charged again. Branch ordered the Twenty-Eighth North Carolina to join the attack, keeping the Eighteenth North Carolina (the unit that would accidentally fire on Jackson at Chancellorsville) in reserve behind Archer. Colonel James Lane of the Twenty-Eighth North Carolina told his men to give the "Rebel Yell." The Eighteenth was behind a ridge near some straw stacks, in a stubble field. "The corn was visible from these straw stacks, to the Antietam, as we approached," wrote one soldier.[203]

Fairchild's three New York regiments were in retreat by the time the Eighth Connecticut was advancing to their farthest point and was met by Branch's brigade. The Eighth did not retreat in the direction they had come, likely because Branch's North Carolinians were now to their south, so they moved northeast, eventually reaching the sheltered area of the road near the Otto and Sherick farmhouses. At one point, Captain Wolcott Marsh said, they "halted and blazed away" at the Confederates. Reaching the ravine and road, they caught their breath and fell back behind other troops. Captain Charles Coit noted, "Our flags are safe but full of holes. All but one of the color guards were shot + the colors were down several times but up they would go again."[204]

General James J. Archer was ill and arrived from Harpers Ferry in an ambulance. Once on the scene, he mounted his horse to lead his brigade. Only about 350 men were with Archer, having lost many stragglers on the "long and fatiguing march." They were directed to the left by A.P. Hill along the Harpers Ferry Road, about 300 yards from Toombs's brigade. They entered a cornfield in front of them and then moved into a plowed field on the other side with a stone fence, under fire the entire time. The Union troops ahead of them were firing from behind the stone wall on the western edge of the forty-acre cornfield. The Tennesseans lost one-third of their number in the distance of 250 yards to the stone wall.[205]

Robert Mockbee of the Fourteenth Tennessee noted that Hill's division recaptured a battery that had fallen into Union hands (McIntosh's). They "charged across an open field," beyond which was a "stone fence" where the three New York units held out. Driving the enemy from it, Colonel William McComb of the Fourteenth Tennessee was seriously wounded, and Lieutenant Colonel J.W. Lockert took over the regiment.[206]

Historian Ezra Carman, who assisted in the establishment of the battlefield park, suggested that some of Archer's losses were friendly fire from Gregg's men, firing through the cornfield as they couldn't see that the Thirtieth Ohio had retreated. Archer's men then took shelter at the wall they had captured. Here the troops fired at the retreating Union soldiers through the wooden fence rails that lined the stone wall.[207]

Colonel Peter Turney, called Old Pete, of the First Tennessee rose up on the fence "as bold as a lion" and yelled, "Hog drivers, advance!" He then leaped over and ran through the corn until he came to the brow of a hill and saw enemy behind a rock wall. In this advance, Archer's brigade lost as many or more than Branch's, an overlooked part of the battle. A Tennessee soldier said of firing on the retreating troops that they "picked them off with unerring aim by the score before they got out of range."[208]

While these events unfolded to the front, at about four thirty, the Ninth New Hampshire witnessed the forward units falling back. Some of the Zouaves of the Ninth New York came crashing through their line, causing confusion. As the New Yorkers charged by, a Confederate shell slammed into the fence behind which the Ninth New Hampshire was sheltering. In an instant, the top fence rail was tossed into the air and whirled end over end above the heads of the New York Zouaves, who ducked in terror. Amazingly, no one was hit by the eight-foot-long projectile.[209]

Lieutenant Colonel Hiram Appleman of the Eighth Connecticut told the color-bearer to not leave, and he responded in the affirmative. In succession, four men fell carrying the national flag. The entire color guard was killed or wounded. Private Charles H. Walker grabbed the flag, planted it in the ground and shook it out defiantly. Then Appleman was hit, and Major John E. Ward assumed command. Men continued to go down, and with no help in sight, Ward saw they were in a desperate situation. Afterward, he wrote that they held their advanced position until ordered back by Rodman, shortly before that officer was killed.[210]

Nineteen-year-old Second Lieutenant Marvin Wait, bright, enthusiastic and well-liked, was one of those hit. He "was seen closing up the ranks and deliberately dressing the line." Wounded and told to go to the rear, he stayed instead and was hit several more times.[211]

Major Ward of the Eighth Connecticut wrote that they "lost over 50 percent of our regiment. The fire from artillery and musketry was very severe, the regiment receiving fire in front and on both flanks." The Eighth retired, hit in front by Toombs's and Kemper's brigades and on their left by Branch's.[212]

Sweeping back the New Englanders were the combined forces of Toombs, Archer and Branch. Toombs and Archer advanced from Harpers Ferry Road to the west, yelling and leaping over the fence, while Branch's North Carolinians came up from the south. Together, they recovered McIntosh's guns and drove the Connecticut troops back. Yet another Union force was arriving, an example of events in one area flowing into another.[213]

Sunset was at six fifteen that evening, and as the shadows grew long and light faded over the rolling terrain, hundreds of exhausted men lay down. Many had been separated from their units and spent the night in small groups or alone. In front of the Seventh Virginia, Private David E. Johnston counted thirty-five dead from the Eighth Connecticut.[214]

Chapter 5

AT THE STONE WALL

As the Eighth Connecticut withdrew in the face of Branch's, Archer's and Toombs's charge, they encountered fresh Union troops as Colonel Eliakim P. Scammon's Kanawha division entered the fray, though its two brigades did so separately. Moving up in the wake of the withdrawal of Harland and the Eighth Connecticut, Colonel Hugh Ewing of the Thirtieth Ohio led a three-regiment brigade consisting of the Twelfth, Twenty-Third and Thirtieth. Lieutenant Henry Brinkerhoff of the Thirtieth Ohio wrote that after crossing Antietam Creek, they reached the summit of the hill and endured a tremendous artillery bombardment.

The men of the Twenty-Third Ohio, like several other units, did not have breakfast that morning and fought the battle on empty stomachs. Having crossed the creek at the ford in the bend of the creek, the regiment was hunkered down above the bridge, waiting to advance with the rest of the corps. Nineteen-year-old Commissary Sergeant William McKinley took the initiative and performed an act that became legendary.

On the east side of the creek, McKinley gathered stragglers in the rear, put them to making coffee and loaded two wagons with the beverage and warm food. Crossing the bridge under artillery fire, he guided the supplies uphill to where the Twenty-Third Ohio was deployed in a line of battle. Soon cheering erupted from the left of the regiment. Colonel Eliakim P Scammon investigated the cause and found McKinley serving the hot coffee and food to the men on the line. He was making his way along, personally supplying each soldier.[215]

Map of troop positions at 5:30 p.m. *Hal Jespersen.*

This was an incredible boost to morale and earned McKinley high praise, as well as one of the most impressive monuments on the battlefield, dedicated in 1903. This helped launch his political career after the war, as he served fourteen years in Congress, twice as governor of Ohio and as a two-term president, starting in 1897.

Ewing's brigade waited in the rear between Otto Lane and the bridge as Fairchild and Harland went forward. They then advanced, the Twelfth Ohio veering south to face a suspected Confederate threat, while the Twenty-Third and Thirtieth moved over broken terrain to the relative safety of the Otto farm lane. Here they crouched down behind a stone wall as Confederate artillery continued to fall in and among them. While moving, the Twelfth Ohio was hit by friendly fire from "raw Connecticut troops," the Sixteenth.

Samuel Compton wrote that "they did not desist till Sargt Snook ran down through the storm of grape and bullets." The Ohioans then laid down in Otto Lane for cover from the Confederate artillery fire. Compton wrote, "My comrade on the right had his brain scattered over me and my nearest on the left had his shoulder blade broken by a…grapeshot."[216]

Ewing's men were waiting for about thirty minutes, and then Colonel Scammon moved them forward at "double quick" to a stone wall along a ridge to their front (later the park tour road, Branch Avenue). Here the Twenty-Third Ohio joined them on their right, and the Twelfth Ohio advanced behind on their left. Henry Brinkerhoff of the Thirtieth Ohio noted that they advanced through a field that was soft, where the "plowed ground gave way under the feet of the men as they ran and when they reached the wall many of the men were worn out with fatigue."[217]

J.E. Walton of the regiment recalled that the "audacity of the move so dumbfounded the enemy that we met but little opposition until we reached the bottom of the depression." They continued up to a stone wall with a rail fence at the crest (Branch Avenue). Walton also noted that the men complained of having smoothbore muskets, which were "not very dangerous if you aimed at anything."

Walton saw that the "rebel line lay across the valley or depression lying between our line and the town of Sharpsburg, and about 400 yards distant." With Fairchild's advance, "Things had assumed a pretty favorable aspect." But not for long.[218]

Major George H. Hildt of the Thirtieth Ohio noted that the Twenty-Third was on their right and Twelfth Ohio on the left as they charged uphill through a twenty-acre cornfield and reached a stone wall, "utterly exhausted." Here they began to fire—slowly at first, but they increased their rate, firing twelve or fifteen times.[219]

The Ohioans could not know what was going on around them as they could not see beyond their right and left; the men were "blissfully ignorant" and "kept popping away" at the enemy to their front. J.E. Walton of the Thirtieth Ohio (about three hundred strong) noted that they were "ensconced behind a stone wall" and fired smoothbore muskets, which were not as accurate as rifles and which the unit was unhappy about. The weapons must have been of poor quality, for the men also struggled to load after firing only five shots; they could "scarcely ram" charges down.[220]

The Twenty-Third Ohio joined them here on their right, but the Twelfth did not keep pace. At the stone wall, the men of the Twenty-Third and the Thirtieth began firing on the Confederates to their front and their left—

Along a stone wall here, the Twenty-Third and Thirtieth Ohio made a stand against Branch's North Carolinians. *Author.*

Brinkerhoff estimated for about twenty minutes. They were suddenly now at the front line and must have felt secure behind their stone wall. Color Sergeant Nathan J. White inspired the unit by jumping up onto the stone wall and waving the flag. At this point, Gregg's brigade entered the forty-acre cornfield to their left and engaged the Sixteenth Connecticut (described in the next chapter).[221]

Alexander Wight of the Twenty-Third Ohio described the protection afforded by the wall, saying, "It served well as a fort and but few killed although a great many more were wounded in their arms and hands, some in the shoulder." The Ohioans exchanged fire from their stone fortress with Archer's and Toombs's brigades, about six hundred yards away. After the war, veterans felt that they could have held this position indefinitely had they not been flanked

The Twenty-Third Ohio hit Branch's North Carolinians, causing them to fall back about one hundred yards. The Seventh and Thirty-Seventh North Carolina advanced again, wheeled to the right and advanced right up to the stone wall, with General Branch among them.[222]

"We were brought under a heavy fire," said one soldier of the Twenty-Third Ohio, "which is a very unpleasant position to be in." The Thirtieth Ohio lost both of its color-bearers here as it occupied the stone wall and straddled the draw through which the Eighth Connecticut had advanced earlier. The desperate Ohioans loaded and fired over their dead and wounded. A soldier of the Twenty-Third wrote, "The rebels were seen coming down upon us, but were mistaken for our men, they having our flag flying and was dressed in our uniform."[223]

Major James Comly of the Twenty-Third Ohio wrote of what happened next, as the Thirtieth took fire on their left from Gregg's South Carolinians. At first, Comly thought they were firing on their own men:

> *About the same time I discovered that the Thirtieth Regiment was still in the corn-field, and that they had opened fire upon what I supposed was our own troops, advancing from the left. It seems proper to state that this supposition did not rest entire upon the fact that the enemy and uniforms similar to ours, and which (I have since been informed by a prisoner) were taken at Harpers Ferry, but upon the fact that they used the national colors on the occasion.*[224]

Having repelled of the Sixteenth Connecticut, Gregg's South Carolinians advanced north, toward the isolated Thirtieth Ohio. At first, Comly thought these were Union reinforcements but was soon convinced otherwise. Colonel Ewing told Comly to change the regiment's facing, from west to south, an extremely difficult maneuver given the circumstances. Only the four right companies heard the order above the din and made the movement. The remining six companies held fast to the wall firing at Archer and Toombs.

At the same time, General Branch swung his troops through a clover field and hit the Twenty-Third Ohio in the left flank. The Thirty-Seventh North Carolina charged up to the Twenty-Third Ohio at the stone fence. An officer in the Twenty-Third described: "A heavy enfilading fire was opened upon our whole line, when I received orders…to change front perpendicularly to the rear"—a rare and complicated maneuver, not easily done in combat. The Twenty-Third Ohio fell back down into the ravine behind them, turned to face directly south and exchanged fire with Gregg's South Carolinians. A few survivors of the Sixteenth Connecticut joined them there. The Ohioans then retreated to the top of the hill where, at Otto's Lane, they sought shelter with other units. Captain William Morris of the Thirty-Seventh North Carolian wrote to his wife, "We whipped them badly with little loss." And in fact, the regiment had only four men wounded.[225]

Branch's North Carolinians and Gregg's South Carolinians were now firing onto the exposed left flank of the Thirtieth Ohio. At the same time, Archer's Tennesseans and Toombs's Georgians advanced against them from the front. Lieutenant Colonel Theodore Jones ordered the regiment to adjust, and he moved to the endangered left but was too far forward and was captured as the Confederates closed in to the wall. In the din and confusion, only some of the regiment heard the order to adjust their position, and those who did tried to move, but the majority of the regiment broke under the pressure.

"The balls flew like hail through the corn," wrote Brinkerhoff of the Thirtieth Ohio. Color Sergeant Nathan White with the national flag was one of the last to abandon the stone wall and was killed before he could get away. Sergeant William Carter was also killed with the regimental flag. Corporals Samuel Howerth and William Buckhannon rescued the flags and bore them in the retreat. Buckhannon had to pry the regimental flag out of Carter's hands, so firm was his grip in death. The National flag had fourteen holes by the end of the day.[226]

The Confederates closed in, up to the wall, and some of Archer's Tennesseans scrambled over it, capturing the wounded Lieutenant Colonel Theodore Jones of the Thirtieth Ohio. Major George Hildt took command, but the Union troops were collapsing. J.E. Walton and his comrades of the Thirtieth Ohio saw the Confederates moving in behind them in the valley. "Making a rush," he wrote, they ran for it, in the process "knocking some of them down with clubbed muskets, and then scattering like a flock of quail each fellow hunted for any tall timber that might chance to be growing."[227]

Ewing also made his way over to the Twenty-Third Ohio, ordering them to reverse direction as well. The regiment did so, swinging south, behind the Thirtieth, to face Gregg's troops. Yet the Confederates were closing in on two sides: Gregg from the south, Archer, Branch and Toombs from the west. When the realization set in, the Buckeyes rushed back, some knocking down Confederate troops in their frenzied dash to safety.

Captain Joseph Clark's Battery E, Fourth U.S. artillery (four ten-pound Parrotts) and Captain George Durell's Independent Battery D, Pennsylvania Light Artillery (six ten-pound Parrotts), deployed along the ridge just above Otto's Lane. They provided much-needed support for the infantry in front but were not immune to incoming fire. Clark wrote, "My First Lt. was killed. My horse killed under me, and I was wounded by a bursting shell. I received four bullets—one through the bridle glove and left thumb, one above the knee joint, one through the thigh and one above the hip of my right leg."[228]

Scammon ordered Colonel Carr B. White to move up the Twelfth Ohio, which remained behind the stone wall at Otto's Lane, with the artillery of both sides flying overhead and occasionally landing among them. The Twelfth moved up to engage Gregg's South Carolinians on the left of the

Union line (the Sixteenth Connecticut and the Fourth Rhode Island had already fallen back). The Ohioans were firing so fast they ran low on ammunition, and participants noted they endured "furious fire" and "nerve racking strain." To make matters worse, a unit behind them fired into the Twelfth, prompting Colonel White to send a messenger to stop it. Caught in the open, receiving murderous fire from Greg's units, and unable to reach the Thirtieth Ohio at the wall, the men of the Twelfth fell back.[229]

The Twenty-Third and the Thirtieth Ohio retreated in different directions, the Twenty-Third moving north and the Thirtieth east uphill to Otto Lane. In the meantime, the other brigade of the Kanawha Division, Crook's, had moved up to Otto's lane near the farmhouse to support Welsh's withdrawing troops. From the start, the two brigades of the division had fought separately, each being attached to other divisions.[230]

The Thirty-Sixth Ohio of Colonel Crook's brigade advanced from Otto's Lane "on the double quick over rolling and ascending ground that had been ploughed and was very rough, and over post and rail fences, so staunch they had to be climbed." Clambering over the fences, several men were picked off by Confederate defenders, and artillery shells rained on them as they

Otto Lane, which shelterd Union troops before and after their attacks to the west. *Author.*

moved into the valley. There in the swale, Lieutenant Colonel Melvin Clarke told the men to lie down, waving his sword to direct them. Just then, a shell struck his right thigh at the hip, and he fell, dying in seconds. He had been in command only ten days and was quite popular with the troops. Crook was nearby and was nearly killed as well.[231]

Crook wrote of their movement,

> *Finally the order for the charge was given, but the moment we raised the crest of the thill and were in full view, we were met with such a hail of musketry bullets, with several batteries dealing death and destruction amongst our ranks, that would seem nothing could survive it.*[232]

Crook took over from Clarke and led the regiment directly. Venturing forward out of the ravine, the Ohioans moved up to a stone fence along a ridge, in line with and north of the Twenty-Third and Thirtieth Ohio (now Branch Avenue), where they could see the fighting to their left and right. They held this line until the general withdrawal. The Twenty-Eighth Ohio was on their left and the already battered Eleventh Ohio in reserve. Nearby, the Eighth Connecticut was gathering after their repulse to the southwest, having retreated all the way to the vicinity of the Sherrick and Otto farms.[233]

At the wall, Crook noted, "We had our hands so full that we knew but little of what was going on elsewhere." With the fighting ending and darkness gathering, Crook withdrew his units back to Otto Lane. The Kanawha division had fought as two separate brigades, and even its regiments fought separately, dispersing the manpower of the division. The Thirtieth Ohio lost eighty men, the most of any unit in Ewing's brigade or the Kanawha Division as a whole, and the Twenty-Third, in line next to them at the stone wall, lost sixty-nine, the second-highest division loss.[234]

Marker for the site of Branch's wounding. *Author.*

The Twenty-Third Ohio's flag was badly shot up, "a curiosity," wrote one soldier of the unit. He noted that the "whole of the blue field, except the last row of stars, is shot away, and the flag is completely in ribbons." Color Sergeant Joshua Armstrong was killed at the wall with the banner. The

Thirtieth's flag had fourteen holes shot through it. General Cox noted that the Ohioans fought with "unflinching tenacity" at the stone wall. Having secured the ground and driven back Fairchild, the Eighth Connecticut and Ewing, the Confederates took shelter behind the stone wall as darkness began to descend.[235]

Across the valley, General A.P. Hill called together Archer, Gregg and Branch to confer near the southern end of the stone wall in the fading light. Suddenly Branch was hit, killed instantly by a bullet; the site is now marked with an upright cannon. Colonel James H. Lane took command after the general was killed. Branch's enslaved servant Wiley recovered Branch's body that evening and took it back to his family in Raleigh.[236]

While the two Union thrusts (that of Fairchild's New York brigade and the isolated Eighth Connecticut) went forward and then swept back, and before the charge of the Ohio troops, to the south, another action was developing. Unfolding amid head-high corn on an uneven slope, it would be one of the most confused, tragic and controversial of the war.

Chapter 6

THE OTHER CORNFIELD

One of the most celebrated episodes of the entire war was the arrival, in the nick of time, of General Ambrose P. Hill's division to save the day for the Confederates at Antietam. In a made-for-Hollywood moment, the Confederate reinforcements arrived in exactly the right place at exactly the right time. Closer examination reveals that A.P. Hill's late-day counterattack was actually more limited and not as devastating as is generally believed; Hill's entire division lost only 346 men and was engaged for about two hours. Only three of Hill's brigades, those of Gregg, Branch and Archer, even entered the fight. The Confederates, however, did enjoy good artillery superiority here, with twenty-one batteries in place, compared to only four Federal batteries. Hill's entry onto the battlefield had the greatest impact in one particular place: the forty-acre cornfield.[237]

These infantry units, like most in the Army of Northern Virginia, were also severely understrength. They had endured the combat of the Seven Days that summer and then the Second Manassas Campaign and the rapid march into Maryland. After securing the captured garrison and supplies at Harpers Ferry, they made a thirteen-mile march to Sharpsburg, foregoing the usual hourly breaks that such a march entails. There was considerable straggling due to the heat.

Hill's troops departed from Harpers Ferry around seven thirty that morning and reached the battlefield at about three o'clock in the afternoon. Their advance from Harpers Ferry and crossing the Potomac to arrive just in time is key to this story, yet one crucial question that has never been

General A.P. Hill. *Library of Congress.*

satisfactorily answered is how the division got over a prominent but often forgotten obstacle: the Chesapeake and Ohio Canal. The C&O Canal ran the entire length of the Potomac River along the north shore. It was about sixty feet wide and nearly six feet deep. On the northern edge of the canal was a twelve foot wide towpath.[238]

Approaching from Pack Horse Ford (also known as Botelor's Ford or Blackburn's Ford), the troops would have encountered the steep earthen wall of the canal, then the water and then the other side with the towpath. Did they build an embankment and fill in the canal to get through? Or cut the canal down and drain the water to get through? Accounts are silent, but one or the other must have been done to make the ford passable. It was a massive obstacle and had to be overcome by either clambering over it or cutting it down. Either option would have been physically challenging, yet no accounts mention how the crossing was done. General William Pendleton only wrote vaguely that "improvements" were made.[239]

Andrew B. Wardlow of the Fourteenth South Carolina described hearing the distant cannon fire as they reached Pack Horse Ford to cross the Potomac. Hill himself arrived at around two thirty, ahead of his division, and rode toward Sharpsburg to consult with General Lee about where to deploy his troops. In his report, Hill stated that his men marched seventeen miles, but the actual distance was thirteen. They did it in about eight hours, a slow but steady pace. The usual ten-minute break every hour was not taken, and there was considerable straggling due to the heat. Hill met with Lee, who told him where to deploy his troops.[240]

The division marched up a now gone road straight up from the ford and then turned right (east) to the Miller Sawmill Road. Colonel O.E. Edwards of the Thirteenth South Carolina noted that they crossed Pack Horse Ford at 2:00 p.m. and arrived on the battlefield at 3:40. The unit was on Gregg's left as they advanced into the cornfield.[241]

As Gregg's troops, the first to enter the fray, advanced, their field of vision was limited by the cornfield in their front and the folds of the ground to their right. How they knew where to go is not recorded; perhaps a staff officer

Pack Horse Ford. *Library of Congress.*

guided them, or maybe it was simple luck that put them at the exact spot they were needed.

The three brigades of Hill's division that entered the fight had about 2,000 men combined, giving each brigade roughly 650 men or each regiment about 170. Gregg's South Carolinians moved from the Harpers Ferry Road downhill toward the unsuspecting troops of the Fourth Rhode Island and Sixteenth Connecticut in a cornfield.

Lieutenant Colonel Reuben L. Walker's artillery battalion preceded Hills' marching infantry and, on arrival, deployed and opened fire. The battalion consisted of several batteries: Braxton's (two three-inch ordnance rifles, four six-pounders), Pegram's (two ten-pound Parrotts, two Napoleons), Mcintosh's (Pee Dee Artillery; one ten-pound Parrott, one three-inch ordnance, one twelve-pound Napoleon, one twelve-pound Howitzer) and Crenshaw's (one twelve-pound Napoleon, one twelve-pound howitzer, two six-pound guns); it had quite the variety.

Three of A.P. Hill's brigades played crucial roles: with Gregg routing two regiments in the forty-acre cornfield and those of Branch and Archer stopping the Eighth Connecticut. His other three brigades were not engaged: Thomas's remained at Harpers Ferry, and Pender's and Brockenbrough's brigades were sent to the far right to protect that flank. Hill moved rapidly to get his units into the fight, at one point encountering a second lieutenant crouching behind a tree. Hill was so mad that he took his sword and broke it over him.[242]

Colonel James H. Lane of Branch's brigade wrote of the "rapid and fatiguing march" from Harpers Ferry. The brigade deployed with the Seventh and Thirty-Seventh North Carolina moving northeast to engage the Eighth Connecticut. General Hill detached the Twenty-Eighth North Carolina to the left on the Harpers Ferry Road, where they were not engaged.[243]

Author Stephen Sears describes the action here in his notable book *Landscape Turned Red*, and his words are worth repeating here: the "cornfield was a particularly nasty place for a fight. There was hardly a level spot in it." The ground slopes down and has numerous rises and dips. Filled with head-high corn, it would have been even worse. For raw troops with no experience, thrust forward into a place they had never seen and into terrain that was hard to see in and around, it was a dangerous situation. The field, described as forty acres, was actually closer to thirty-eight—much larger than Miller's better-known cornfield on the north end of the battlefield, though certainly lesser known and not nearly as deadly. But it would be deadly enough. The cornfield, owned by Joseph Sherrick and leased to Leonard Emmert, was about to become the center of fighting.[244]

At about four thirty, as Fairchild's New York brigade advanced "under a tremendous fire from the enemy's batteries" and drove them from the stone wall, Fairchild observed A.P. Hill's arrival on the left and called on Rodman to bring up Harland's brigade. His four regiments were spread out over a wide area, all out of support of each other. The Eighth was already far in advance, alongside Fairchild's New Yorkers; the Sixteenth had entered the forty-acre cornfield and laid down; and the Fourth Rhode Island was behind them coming up. The Eleventh Connecticut was misled by an aide and did not advance as required. Their absence meant that Harland had only three regiments, and the Sixteenth was a totally inexperienced unit on the army's left flank.[245]

Colonel Edward Harland noted that the Sixteenth

> *apparently did not hear the order. I sent an aide to order them forward. This delay on the left placed the Eighth considerably in advance of the rest of the brigade. I asked Gen. Rodman if I should halt the Eighth, and wait for the rest of the brigade. He ordered me to advance the Eighth, and he would hurry up the Sixteenth Connecticut and 4th Rhode Island.*

Then, seeing Gregg's advance toward the vulnerable left flank, Harland realized the danger and "put spurs to my horse to hasten up the Sixteenth Connecticut." He also sent Major Lyon to alert Rodman and Fairchild of the impending danger.[246]

Rodman would have barely been able to see the advance of Gregg's Brigade over the crest to the south of his location. He rode down to the cornfield and briefly consulted with Colonel Beach about adjusting to meet the threat and then rode back toward Fairchild, but he never made it. Rodman fell mortally wounded behind the Eighth Connecticut's position.

Gregg's view as his units entered the cornfield, which was in the middle ground here. *Author.*

His loss came at a crucial time for the Union forces. Harland's horse was hit, and he continued on foot, taking over command of the two brigades.[247]

Fighting in their first battle, the men and officers of the Sixteenth Connecticut had not yet acquired that crucial but hard-earned skill that veterans possessed: battlefield sense, or knowing what is going on around them, where to be, how to prepare and anticipate and how to maneuver through difficult terrain, all while maintaining awareness of the location of friendly and hostile units around them. The unit had been in service for only a month; most of the men barely knew the basics of maneuver and how to fire their weapons. The unwieldy new regiment also had more men (about seven hundred) than Gregg's entire approaching brigade of five regiments.[248]

The rolling terrain here made it difficult to see in any given direction and hampered communication. What happened next was swift and deadly for the New Englanders, who had no idea danger was so near until they head the "rustling of cornstalks."[249]

Samuel McGovan of Gregg's brigade thought they arrived at about 3:40 p.m. The Fourteenth South Carolina was in the lead, and Gregg sent them to the right to guard that flank. The First, Twelfth and Thirteenth Regiments formed and entered the field from the high ground to the west. The Thirteenth South Carolina was on the left behind a stone fence. The Twelfth advanced downhill into the corn, directly into the Sixteenth Connecticut. The First went forward on their right. Being in front, the First and Twelfth regiments did the bulk of the fighting and took most of the casualties. The Twelfth even lost a few prisoners, attesting to the close-quarters fighting and dispelling the notion that the action was one-sided.[250]

The Fourteenth South Carolina had moved off the Harpers Ferry Road and down the slope toward a stone wall at the western edge of the cornfield. Captain Joseph N. Brown of the Fourteenth South Carolina noted that they were on the brigade's right, were "not actively engaged" and suffered no losses. The unit drifted to the southeast, well below the fighting in the cornfield. The Twelfth and the First bore the brunt of the fighting. One company of the Sixteenth Connecticut had advanced to the western edge of the cornfield as skirmishers but were quickly overrun by Gregg's approaching veterans. The troops from the Palmetto State had been able to replace their smoothbore muskets with state-of-the-art Springfield rifles at Harpers Ferry.[251]

Colonel Daniel H. Hamilton, First South Carolina, wrote of "pressing on over fences and every obstacle, reached a high ridge in a corn-field." Told that the enemy was flanking them, he turned back the three right companies and fired on them. They fired so much that they used up their ammunition and their rifles clogged; some men resorted to using stones to hammer down charges.[252]

Lieutenant Colonel James M. Perrin of the First South Carolina Rifles noted that they were on the right of the First South Carolina when they entered the cornfield. Ascending the crest, they found the enemy on the First's right and fired on them with a "destructive volley." Perrin wrote, "So great was the confusion caused by our fire, this large, well-equipped regiment failed to rally, broke and fled the field in the utmost confusion." Soon after arriving, color-bearer Captain James D. Malone was shot and the flag caught by Private Clinkscales. Lieutenant Colonel Perrin was hit in the throat.[253]

Major William H. McCorkle with the 250-man Twelfth South Carolina described being in the center of the advance, going downhill into the cornfield and the terrible crossfire they endured. In hand-to-hand fighting, a Connecticut soldier seized the Twelfth's flag. Colonel Dixon Barnes caught the staff in his left hand and, with his right, cut down the soldier with his sword. Colonel Barnes was then hit and killed, and McCorkle took command.[254]

At one point, General Gregg and Captain Alexander Haskell rode forward through the corn and emerged just across from a stone wall with Union troops beyond it (a stone wall bordered the western edge of the cornfield, and this would have been to the right of the Sixteenth Connecticut). The soldiers fired and hit Haskell's and Gregg's horses. They wheeled and fled. Gregg was hit by a spent ball and nearly fell from his horse. The other officers helped him dismount once they were out of danger.[255]

Staff officer James Fitz Caldwell of the First South Carolina described the opening assault:

> *Leaving the narrow country road, the brigade was carried over one of the many steep hills that characterize that country, and arranged for battle. The Fourteenth regiment was posted behind a low stone fence, on the right of the brigade, and nearly at right angles with the front of the other regiments. Below us stretched a wide field of luxuriant corn, and beyond it was a clear space with varying breadth out of which rose numerous hills like those…clear of trees. Into the cornfield the First, Twelfth, and Thirteenth regiments were advanced in line of battle, to drive the enemy. The line reached the top of a small eminence in the cornfield, and soon engaged the Federal line moving through the corn. The Thirteenth regiment held a stone fence on the left. Col. Barnes, with the Twelfth regiment, charged the enemy,*

driving him rapidly from the stone fence he occupied just beyond.... There was some difference of opinion at this time as to Gen. Gregg's orders, Col. Edwards regarding them as defensive, Col. Barnes as offensive. I am not able to say which was right. Col. Hamilton advanced the First regiment nearly abreast with the Twelfth. But the Twelfth soon outflanked itself by its rapid dash into the enemy's line, and had to be withdrawn a space. After a little time, however, Col. Barnes returned to the attack, and this time drove away the force which had occupied the fence on his retirement, pursuing them to the opposite hill and inflicting a heavy loss upon them.

A considerable pressure was now brought to bear upon the right of the First regiment. Col. Hamilton changed his front slightly to meet it, and swept the obnoxious line from the field, with great loss to it. This movement also secured Col. Barnes' right from further molestation. Hardly, however, had it been executed, when a line of Federals came hurrying down on the right of the First regiment, threatening soon to enfilade their line. Gen. Gregg now despatched Capt. Perrin with Orr's Rifles after them. The Rifles fell upon this line, almost completely flanking the flankers, and after a short, sharp fire, dispersed them in irretrievable order.[256]

Lieutenant Bernard F. Blakeslee of the Sixteenth wrote in his diary,

While we were lying here, we were suddenly ordered to Attention! When a terrible volley was fired into us from behind a stone wall about five rods [about ninety feet] *in front of us. We were ordered to fix bayonets and advance. In a moment we were riddled with shot. Many necessary orders were given which were not understood. Neither the line-officers nor the men had any knowledge of regimental movements.*[257]

"The most helpless confusion ensued. Our men fell by scores on every side," wrote Blakeslee. Putting the best face on it, he went on, "Still our position was obstinately maintained, until ordered to fall back." Adjutant John H. Burnham, writing to his mother, said, "We got the best of it on the whole."[258]

Private Edwin B. "Ned" Lillie of the Sixteenth noted that they were lying down in a cornfield with shells passing overhead. The enemy arrived suddenly, and "before we could get into position gave us a terrible volley from behind a stone wall not five rods away." The New Englanders rose and fixed bayonets and then were ordered to advance. Officers and men fell all around him, and few understood the orders given as they were

This marker notes that General Rodman was mortally wounded 365 yards to the south, at the time a spot that was not part of the park. *Author.*

new to combat and maneuvering. "The enemy saw our disorder and drove down upon us."[259]

They were ordered to fall back, but Lillie was hit in the leg, breaking it just above the ankle, and he went down as his comrades swept past. Feeling "faint," Lillie "knew nothing of what was passing around me." The Confederates were nearby at a stone wall, and firing went on for a few more hours. Bandaging his wound with his handkerchief, Lillie looked around and saw dead and wounded all around him in the corn. A few feet away, he recognized John Loveland, wounded in the leg and unconscious from loss of blood. Ned crawled over to him, gave him the last of the water from his canteen and bandaged his leg with John's handkerchief. John regained consciousness but said little, being in great pain. Darkness descended on the valley, and Ned lay there amid cries for water and help. He would lie there all through the next day without water or help until his unit found him on September 19.[260]

Men who had only loaded their rifles once were desperately trying to load and fire at an unseen enemy in the head-high corn. Adrenaline pulsed through their veins, and stress overwhelmed many. Volleys from Gregg's troops tore into them from just a few feet in front. Then they were seen to raise a United States flag and call out, "Don't fire on friends." A Connecticut veteran wrote, "The position was so exposed that we were ordered to fall back, which was rapidly done."[261]

Colonel Francis Beach was on a white horse at the time. So unprepared were the troops that their flags were still cased. Flags were not only important for morale but also served as guides during the chaos of battle. Sergeant Major Robert Kellogg described the attack as "one of the most terrific

The view of the Sixteenth Conneticut, at the time in a head-high cornfield. *Author.*

volleys of musketry that I think was ever poured into a Regt. Our men fell on every side.…You can have no idea of it; it was like a hail storm."[262]

An officer yelled out to Beach in desperation, "Tell us what you want us to do and we'll try to obey you." He replied, "I want my men to face the enemy." As they stumbled and attempted to move, the rookie soldiers encountered a wooden fence. Some officers yelled, "Tear down the fence"; others ordered, "Never mind the fence," all amid the incoming rifle fire. Adding to the confusion was the "hideous rebel yell."[263]

What soldiers saw and experienced in Sherrick's cornfield depended on where they were in the line. Some of the Connecticut soldiers on the right of their line would have seen Confederates close to the stone wall at the upper (west) end of the cornfield. Those in the center and left were downslope and likely saw very little of the enemy.

Jacob Bauer wrote to his wife Sarah that they "got pretty well mixed up & when in this position the rebels came upon us flying our own flag till their muskets touched our very faces…this put us in utter confusion and the devils advanced until our very noses touched theirs." During the engagement, Bauer was side by side with his friend George Chamberlain, whom he had not seen since. Chamberlain was in fact badly wounded and would succumb to his wounds three years later.[264]

In the confusion unfolding in the cornfield, one Connecticut soldier wrote that "men were falling before me, behind, and on both sides." Another wrote that the Confederate's "fire was terrible and the ground was covered with dead and wounded, we had to fall back or all be taken prisoners." "It is a wonder that anyone got away, " said a third. Another soldier wrote to a friend that the Confederates' fire was "terrible and the ground was covered with dead & wounded. We had to fall back or all be taken prisoners."[265]

A soldier noted that the Confederates were only about one hundred feet away firing at them. Another wrote, "A skedaddle became general. The yells of the rebs were awful and the tune of the bullets whistled by my ears is never to be forgotten. It is wonderful how I escaped unharmed." The retreat "was accomplished in Bull Run fashion," noted Jacob Bauer.[266]

Adjutant John H. Burnham of the Sixteenth wrote,

> *We were in a field of thick heavy corn where you could not see twelve feet ahead and things were somewhat mixed at times.…All at once looking up to the left I saw a rebel brigade which had outflanked us so prettily forming with the utmost order and coolness.…I am frank to confess that although I had no idea of running away, I trembled. You may call the*

> *feeling fear or anything you chose for I don't deny that I trembled and wished were well out of it.*[267]

Private Aretas Culver said that the Confederates "treacherously displayed the U.S. colors" and that they called out not to fire on their own men.

> *At that point of attack, they lowered their standards and hoisted the rebel ensign in its place, then it was the Acting Brig. Gen. Harland* [who] *ordered Col. Beach to change position to escape their deadly cross-fire; Co. B. attempted it, but in vain, and he was obliged to report to his superior that his regiment had never had a battalion drill, but one dress parade and scarcely new how to form in a line-of-battle.*[268]

Sixteen-year-old Wells Bigham was in the cornfield with his brother John, who was killed. Wells wrote to his father, "They had our uniforms and flags so we thought they were all right." Eighteen-year-old Corporal Samuel B. Mettler recalled,

> *We saw them advancing and supposed they were our men, as they were dressed just like us, but we soon found out the truth. Before we could form, they were upon us, and though they encountered a heavy fire, yet being nearly 5,000 to 800 of us, drove us back behind our batteries.*

Mettler was grazed by a bullet as he ran and recalled that "the men were so scarred, they fled in all directions."[269]

Sergeant William H. Relyea stated matter-of-factly, "I very quickly decided it was no place for me," and he joined in the scramble backward. Nearby, Private Austin D. Thompson said, "The bullets flew so thick that the Reg. was all confused and after one or two rallys, were forced to retreat."[270]

Private Elizur D. Belden wrote of "a scene of terror, every man for himself." He "turned with the rest and made for the fence" behind them but was hit in the thigh and "crawled along through the shower of bullets to a small gutter where I now lay down, several others lay down with me, the bullets & shells flew over me thick and fast. There I lay not daring to stir until dark when the firing ceased." Private John B Cuzner said, "As for myself, I am a big coward," and he "ran when they gave the order to retreat," eventually hiding behind a stone wall. Cuzner said that the unit was "cut to pieces most shockingly."[271]

Other soldiers spoke of not being able to see anything in the cornfield and the Confederates using a "National colors" and having "on our clothes." Private George Robbins wrote to his sister, "I did not run until the rest did." Corporal Sidney Hayden wrote to his father,

> *We were ordered into a cornfield…and the Rebels got close on to us by dressing in our clothes and carrying our flag firing volley after volley on us while we supposed* [they] *were our friends and tried to stop them without firing a shot ourselves until they were discovered.*[272]

Colonel Francis Beach managed to rally some of his Sixteenth men with the Eleventh Connecticut, but they were badly scattered and many were entirely gone. Lieutenant Colonel Frank Cheney and Major George A. Washburn were wounded, and three captains and a lieutenant were killed. Corporal Francis Latimer saved the regiment's flag from capture during the chaos and was promoted to color sergeant for the act.[273]

John B. Cuzner wrote more of his odyssey: "I ran behind a tree and looking around saw my Captain running for another tree's protection, thought I'd follow him, after a moment's rest off he went again and took shelter behind a clump of bushes and then an old stump." He followed Captain Edward Mix "until we had the shelter of the stone wall between us and the firing. In this retreat, as long as I was following my Captain's flying coat tails I felt I was all right and it would have been laughable had it not been extremely serious."[274]

The Fourth Rhode Island, which had been under artillery fire ever since crossing Antietam Creek, was slightly back from the Sixteenth Connecticut and advanced up when the Confederates struck. George Allen noted that Colonel Harland ordered them to move down from the hill at Otto's Lane and into a cornfield in which the Sixteenth Connecticut had advanced. As they did so, the incoming artillery fire continued. In the ranks of the Fourth was Private Calixa Lavallee, a French Canadian who had moved to the United States before the war. He would be wounded in the leg before the day was over. After the war, Lavallee composed the Canadian National Anthem, "O Canada."[275]

The Fourth Rhode Island was a veteran unit but had only a few officers to manage the regiment. Colonel William Steere sent Lieutenant Colonel Joseph Curtis to the Sixteenth Connecticut to ask them to join in a charge. Making his way amid the confusion, high corn and uneven ground, he found that the other unit "was badly broken, and a little later under the impulse of the enemy's heavy fire, and possibly seeing what we also soon saw, retreated to the rear, breaking heavily through the right of our regiment." This in turn left the Rhode Islanders alone with no support.[276]

Curtis "found the Sixteenth Ct giving way and crowding upon its right compelling" the Fourth Rhode Island "to move to left, rendering it almost impossible to dress the line." All the while, incoming Confederate fire was taking its toll. Curtis yelled out to Steere, "We must depend on ourselves."[277]

George Allen explained the movement of the Fourth Rhode Island:

> *Descending into the valley to its support, it found the Sixteenth Connecticut giving way, and crowding upon its right, compelling it to move to the left. It was now subjected to a sharp musket fire from the front, but as the enemy showed the National flag (the corn concealing their uniform), and as our troops had been seen in advance on our right, the order was given to cease firing, and a volunteer officer to go forward to ascertain who was in our front was called for.*[278]

Lieutenants George E. Curtis and George H. Watts moved ahead on either side of Corporal Thomas B. Tanner, who carried the regimental flag. They advanced through the corn to within twenty feet of the Confederates, who then fired, killing Tanner. Curtis seized the flag and raced back, with Watts close behind—both, amazingly, surviving the close encounter. Colonel William Steere then ordered the regiment to fire and sent Allen to the Sixteenth Connecticut to see if they could help in charging against the Confederates.[279]

Returning to Colonel Steere, Allen reported, "We must depend on ourselves." By then, the Confederates had outflanked the New Englanders on their left, with intense rifle fire coming into them. The Rhode Islanders were "standing in this corn field alone and unsupported, and striving their best to keep pegging away at the rebel force in our front, yet not knowing how many or in what position they were." Allen felt that the Confederates were "determined to wipe us out." The confusion was overwhelming: "No one seemed to know the position of the rebel forces, whether in our front, flank, or rear."

With the Sixteenth Connecticut collapsing and crowding into the Rhode Islanders, Colonel William Steere had no choice but to order the unit to move back and to the right. "Confusion reigned supreme for awhile." The movement began orderly enough but soon devolved into confusion. Moving through the cornfield, with the enemy close upon them and the rookie Connecticut soldiers pushing into them, soon caused the Fourth Rhode

Position and view of the Fourth Rhode Island. *Author.*

Island's soldiers to break and run. Colonel Steere was wounded in the left thigh during the retreat.

George Allen later wrote down what was likely a common thought among Union soldiers that day. "This regiment was moved around from one place to another without knowing sometimes, where its position in line was to be or its relative position to the rest of the brigade."

Allen noted that "above us on the hill were the Stars and Stripes, the top of which we could just see over the corn." He ordered, "Cease firing, you are firing up on your own men." Seeing the troops in front of them with a United States flag, the Rhode Islanders assumed they were other Union troops, and orders to cease firing rang out from the officers. Yet there was uncertainty, so a call went out for a volunteer to go forward and find out who was in front of them.[280]

Lieutenant Henry Spooner said that the enemy was in the cornfield

> *where the thick, high grown corn served largely to conceal them from us, but where their position was demonstrated by their sharply challenging rifles. They occupied the crest of one of the numerous small rolling hills,*

> *with which that locality was covered, while we had reached its base. The interchange of fire between us was fierce and rapid, until suddenly there was a lull in their firing and plainly above them and over the waving corn floated our National flag…The cry ran down our line "We are firing on our own men."*[281]

The First South Carolina ended up facing the Fourth Rhode Island, and the New Englanders briefly pushed them back. The First South Carolina Rifles (not to be confused with the First South Carolina) then advanced as the First regiment became low on ammunition and fell back.[282]

One of the more famous incidents of the battle was the confusion caused by some of A.P. Hill's troops wearing captured Union uniforms from Harpers Ferry. Few Confederate accounts give many details about how many troops or which units had them. Has it been exaggerated? Which units had blue coats, and how many troops may have actually worn them? This issue is worth exploring in more detail. Accounts from the Sixteenth Connecticut and the Fourth Rhode Island mention that the enemy in front of them (Gregg's South Carolinians) were in blue, but were there others (Branch's and Archer's men)? Were whole regiments in blue or just part of them? Confederate accounts contain few details, and it is hard to quantify from the evidence we have.

Author Kevin Pawlak has suggested that the Union troops were in a head-high cornfield and looking into the setting sun, which affected their vision. He argues that wearing captured blue uniforms on purpose could have done as much harm as good, since other Confederates might have mistaken them for the enemy and fired into them. These are all valid points, and the fact that before the next battle at Fredericksburg the blue uniforms were ordered to be removed bears this out.[283]

Evidence is slim and conflicting. Very few Southern accounts exist at all from Hill's division or Gregg's brigade. John Keely of the Nineteenth Georgia, in Archer's brigade, wrote, "We were nearly naked" at Harpers Ferry, and "We immediately replenished our wardrobes from those of the enemy." Andrew Wardlaw of the Fourteenth South Carolina noted that the ground was littered with discarded gray uniforms "which our soldiers had thrown off, substituting new ones. I got a good Yankee overcoat for myself and one for Wiley."[284]

Robert Mockbee of the Fourteenth Tennessee noted that, "but for the Tattered Battle flags [we] might have been taken for a brand new Brigade from Boston so completely were they clothed in Yankee uniforms." Yet later he noted that on the march from Harpers Ferry, "many cast off blue garments and the old faded gray coat or jacket took the place of the blue." It is not known how many Confederates had blue uniforms or cast them off or why—or why they would carry their old uniforms on the march. This author has found no other Confederate accounts of wearing blue.[285]

There are too many accounts of the incident for it to have been a mistaken assumption by the New Englanders. It is possible that some men wore the blue uniforms not to trick the Federals but simply to replace worn-out clothing. A.P. Hill's division had no idea where they would enter the battle or how they would be deployed, so to assume that they wore blue to deceive the enemy seems unrealistic. After the war, many Sixteenth Connecticut veterans wrote of the uniforms as a deception, but that may not have been the case. Justifying their poor performance was made easier by describing the trickery of the Confederates in blue.

Several accounts also mention the Southerners having National flags, which seems more unlikely. Captured flags were considered trophies and usually sent to a unit's home state or the War Department. Regiments had a great deal of pride in their own battle flags, making it unlikely the Confederates would have carried those taken at Harpers Ferry. How do we account for these Union claims? Perhaps in the confusion of battle, Confederate flags were mistaken for Union ones. Some South Carolina units also carried blue state or unit flags, which may have resembled the national flag in the haze of battle. In addition, some Confederate units were also carrying First National flags, which also resembled the United States flag.[286]

Colonel Steere saw Confederates three ranks deep (the First South Carolina Rifles) moving in on their left, about one hundred yards away. Anticipating the impending threat, he ordered the regiment to withdraw by the right flank but was immediately hit in the hip and went down, unable to see the maneuver executed. The unit's right companies started to move, but the left companies did not hear it. Seeing those on the right moving, they thought an order to retreat had been given, and they began to break for the rear. The unraveling was impossible for officers to overcome as the South Carolinian's fire continued to pour into them.

Lieutenant Colonel Clark was hit twice, and Second Lieutenant Henry Spooner had two shots pass through his clothing and suffered a contusion on his right hip from a ball hitting his saber, so the unit lost two more important officers at this moment. The regiment fell back and scrambled up the hill toward Otto's Lane. Of the roughly 400 men of the Fourth

Rhode Island who crossed Antietam Creek, 102 were killed and wounded, and seven who couldn't keep up were scooped up as prisoners, a steep loss of 25 percent.[287]

Staff officer James Caldwell of the First South Carolina wrote of the action,

> *The firing during this period, which was about an hour, was as rapid as possible, and on our side unusually accurate. So dense was the corn that the lines sometimes approached within thirty or forty yards of each other before opening. We had somewhat the advantage, for the enemy, descending to attack us, naturally fired too high, which we had either a level or a rise to fire on. I need not explain this, for it is a universally known fact that men fire above their own levels. And when the enemy retreated they had to pass through open ground, which enabled us to kill large numbers of them. But our object was entirely defensive. It was enough, fully enough, for this division to save the right flank of the army....*
>
> *This was an exciting field to view. Far along in front of the Confederate army, on our left, we could see the blue lines of the Federals, moving to the attack over the smooth, round hills, marching in perfect order, with banners flying and guns and bayonets glittering in the sun. Never, even in the regular armies of France and Austria, have I witnessed such accurate marching. And their appearance was greatly improved by their well-kept, loose, blue uniform, which gave them a massive look, entirely unlike the tight, light colored and variegated garb of the Confederates. I could see the skirmishers of the enemy as they exchanged their scattering discharges with the Confederates. Then they would retire upon the main line of battle, then an irregular fire would open on both sides, which would swell until they poured their whole roaring volleys into each other, and the field was wrapped in smoke. After a while the enemy would begin to waver. They would seesaw back and forth, then one and another would give way, the more and more until a whole line would break and fly before the loud hurrahs of our troops....*
>
> *The neat number and height of the hills allowed the hostile batteries to fight each other, even when the lines of infantry were closed to conflict. After the repulse of the last attempt of the enemy, their artillery played upon our infantry and artillery with a slow and pretty good fire.*
>
> *McIntosh's battery...did good service on the left of the division. At one time, no support being given them, they fought the enemy's infantry single-handed, until overwhelmed by numbers and exhausted of ammunition, they were forced to retire with their caissons and limbers. But, before they*

> *did give way, they double-charged their pieces and dealt destruction among the enemy. A member of the battery told me that he counted forty Federal corpses in the group, where the double-shot was discharged. Archer's brigade soon charged the enemy, and recovered the pieces.*[288]

General Maxcey Gregg had about seven hundred men in his whole brigade. Although the seven hundred men of the Sixteenth Connecticut were inexperienced and caught unprepared, their fire was not inaccurate. Colonel Dixon Barnes of the Twelfth South Carolina was killed, while two captains and Captain James Perrin of Orrs Rifles were wounded. Gregg himself was also wounded in the hip, badly bruised by a spent ball that failed to penetrate the skin.[289]

Corporal Berry G. Benson of the First South Carolina recalled:

> *Running rapidly forward through the corn, we stopped at the top of the hill and poured a galling fire into the fleeing foe. Many of them stopped in a little hollow in the corn at the foot of the hill, afraid to attempt the passage of the open slope beyond. Into them grouped here in a crouching disorderly line, we poured volley after volley, doubtless with terrible execution.*

Benson noted,

> *Besides those lying in the ravine, part of the enemy's line had taken refuge behind a stone fence or ridge of rocks which did not appear to protect them fully, for by ones and twos and threes they were continually breaking from it and fleeing across the open slope beyond. These with those who fled the ravine fairly dotted the green slope. And now amongst them, spurring down the hillside, came galloping an officer, mounted on a black horse, waving his sword and endeavoring to rally the scattered line. Our eyes all turned to him, a fair mark, and half a thousand rifles were aimed, and a storm of bullets sped in their mission. Both horse and rider fell….*
>
> *Suddenly and unexpectedly, whilst we were thus having things our own way, came a volley from our flank which drove us back precipitately, and we had hardly chance to deliver a shot ere we were being hotly pursued. I found myself dropping behind, for my pantaloons…proved to be of weak stuff and had already begun to rip at the bottom of the left leg. And now being wet by fording the river, they were heavier, so that the running caused them to spit further and further, so that now every time I threw the left leg forward, the breeches leg flew forward and wrapped around my right leg.*

Bullets whistled around me thick, for I must have been a conspicuous target. A bullet struck me on the right side of the head, leaving a black mark on my gray felt hat. Feeling it strike, I stopped, seized the cloth in my hands and tore the leg off a foot above the knee, and "skedaddled."

Our line did not run far, but jumped into a gully and fronted, awaiting in this natural breastwork the advance of the enemy. But they did not come, nor were we ordered forward. Sitting down there, one of the men asked me if that was a bullet hole in my drawers. Looking down I saw two holes near the bottom of the leg, and unrolling it…I found in all six holes, one bullet having doubtless passed through three folds of the cloth. And so I came out of the battle of Sharpsburg or Antietam half trouserless.[290]

Also in the cornfield was a very frail Lieutenant Archibald McIntyre. A week earlier, he was in a hospital in Virginia with typhoid fever. Learning that the army had invaded Maryland, he made his way north and rejoined the First South Carolina the night before the battle. Advancing with his comrades into the corn, McIntyre was hit and killed.[291]

General Cox moved Sturgis's division up to shore up the line as Rodman's troops fell back. It is not known if Burnside was any nearer to the front than the stone bridge. Ferrero's brigade moved up to Otto Lane, taking cover behind a worm fence. The Thirty-Fifth Massachusetts was on the right and then the Twenty-First from the same state and the Fifty-First Pennsylvania and New York on the left. Here the brigade endured Confederate artillery fire, including railroad iron and other scrap metal. They exchanged fire with Gregg's and Archer's brigades to their front.[292]

Sunset was about six thirty that evening, ending the bloodiest single day in U.S. history. As the air cooled and shadows grew across the rolling terrain, men of both sides settled down, exhausted. No fighting occurred the next day, and on September 19, Lee pulled the Army of Northern Virgina back across the Potomac, leaving the field in Union hands.

Chapter 7

A DISTINGUISHED FIELD

The most remarkable feature of Antietam which distinguishes it from most other battlefields managed by the National Park Service is the almost perfect integrity of the site.
—*Gary T. Scott, National Register Nomination*[293]

The aftermath of battle rarely captures attention as much as the excitement of determined charges and stubborn defenses. Yet how a battle, or any important event, is remembered and commemorated is vitally important. Following the Confederate withdrawal on September 18–19, Union troops buried the dead and cleaned up the debris of battle, a task that was nearly as traumatic as battle for many new units and lived long in the memory of veterans.

The night of September 17 was a long and painful experience for the wounded who lay on the battlefield overnight with no help or water. A cold, drizzling rain fell, adding to the misery of the thousands of men spread out over the hills and fields. That evening, Private Almon L. Reed of the Eighty-Ninth New York lay among the dead and wounded near the Harpers Ferry Road. That afternoon, he had played dead, lying as still as he could, while McIntosh's Battery fired over his head. Reed was "almost buried with the dirt and small stones that had been thrown upon me by the shot which plowed the earth on every side." Lying there all night, he was drenched by the rain. "During the night the Rebels were going through my pockets every few minutes," he wrote. Taken into Sharpsburg in the morning, Union troops found him after occupying the town.[294]

The site of the forty-acre cornfield, with the Sixteenth Connecticut's monument. In the distance is Otto Lane. None of these key areas were acccessible to the public prior to the 2000s. *Author.*

"I shall never forget that night," wrote a wounded soldier in the forty-acre cornfield, "the Johnnies were all about… rifling through the bodies of the dead.…I heard one of them call out 'Are there any of the 16th here?' I asked him if he meant the 16th Conn as I belong to them 'oh the 16th Conn be d—d it's the 16th South Carolina I want' was the sharp rejoinder to my question."[295]

Private Samuel Compton of the Twelfth Ohio stated, "We slept in ranks on the battle field. It was a cool September night. Your bed the ground. Your covering the sky. My teeth chattered in rhythm to my shaking limbs." Getting up around midnight to find a blanket, Compton came across a mound covered with blankets. Removing one, he found it covered two corpses. "Of course I left the blanket alone," he recorded in his diary.[296]

The next day, Edward K. Wightman of the Ninth New York walked over the ground where they charged the day before. "Our dead still lay unburied," wrote, "horribly mangled and lying in every conceivable attitude." He also saw that "fences were everywhere broken done, trees shattered, the ground ploughed up in furrows, and everything testified to the terrible destructiveness of the agencies employed."[297]

David Johnston of the Seventh Virginia noted that in front of Kemper's brigade, the nearest Union dead were only fifty yards away, a testament to how close they had come. He also counted thirty-three dead of the Eighth Connecticut on the ground where Kemper's and Toombs's brigades had counterattacked. Finding a wounded Connecticut soldier, Johnston gave him some water and filled his canteen. The battlefield was quiet but still dangerous on September 18, as a soldier of the Seventh Virginia was killed by a sharpshooter while going forward to assist the Union wounded. Captain James Wren of the Forty-Eighth Pennsylvania noted that on the front line that day, "We ware Compelled to take a stand & take all the protection we Could" and that they "dare not raise our heads."[298]

Seth Plumb of the Eighth Connecticut wrote,

> *I found that every thing had been taken from the pockets of our men and much of their clothing stripped from them. We gathered our dead and brought them away to bury yesterday morning but were ordered away before we could do it.... We left names of all on a piece of paper tied to their clothes.*

Confederate dead on the lower battlefield by Alexander Gardner. *Library of Congress.*

Captain Wolcott Marsh of the Eighth wrote, "I went up where our regit. was engaged & there what a sight. 30 men from our regit. alone lay dead in a little field & nearby was 42 Zouaves [Ninth New York]."[299]

As each grave was dug, the men had time to dwell on the loss. Long hours allowed time for reflection, as opposed to the fast-paced and terrifying minutes of combat. First impressions of combat left lasting memories for the men in new units like the 100th Pennsylvania, Sixteenth Connecticut and Thirty-Fifth Massachusetts. Survivors buried about forty dead of the Sixteenth Connecticut. In the field where they charged, men of the Eighth Connecticut laid their dead to rest, "buried side by side near a large tree on the ridge just above where the gallant charge began." There were also over one hundred dead Confederates in this field.[300]

Adjutant John Burnham of the Sixteenth Connecticut observed that their own dead had their pockets turned out, emptied by Southern scavengers. Captain Robert Kellogg of the unit noted that "we found dead rebels with our unform on."[301]

The dazed and exhausted men of the Sixteenth Connecticut buried their dead, "a very unpleasant duty and made many soldiers sick." Antietam was their first battle and the first time they saw dead comrades. Captain Julian Pomeroy wrote to Sarah Aldrich, whose husband, Henry, had been killed, telling her that they buried him on top of a grassy hill.[302]

The New Englanders buried their forty killed soldiers in blankets and officers in "rude rough boxes" in a mass grave near the forty-acre cornfield, by a large tree and a stone wall. Chaplain Finch and Adjutant John H. Burnham made sure "men of each company laid side by side, and each grave marked so that the bodies could be recovered if desired." It was the best they could do under the conditions.[303]

An 1864 map drawn by cartographer S.G. Elliott and discovered in the spring of 2020 in the New York Public Library shows the location of battlefield burials as well as where dead horses were gathered to be burned. Concentrations of burials are often indicators of areas of heavy fighting. Note the burial trenches along Otto Lane, near the forty-acre cornfield, in the path of Harland's charge and along Confederate defensive positions. Also of note: many burial trenches follow ridges and align with modern terrain, as can be seen when this 1864 map is overlaid on a modern one.[304]

The soldiers of the Ninth New Hampshire spent all day

> *burying our dead and the piles of rebels that lay dead on the ground we gained. At the bridge were piles of men and horses, in heaps together;*

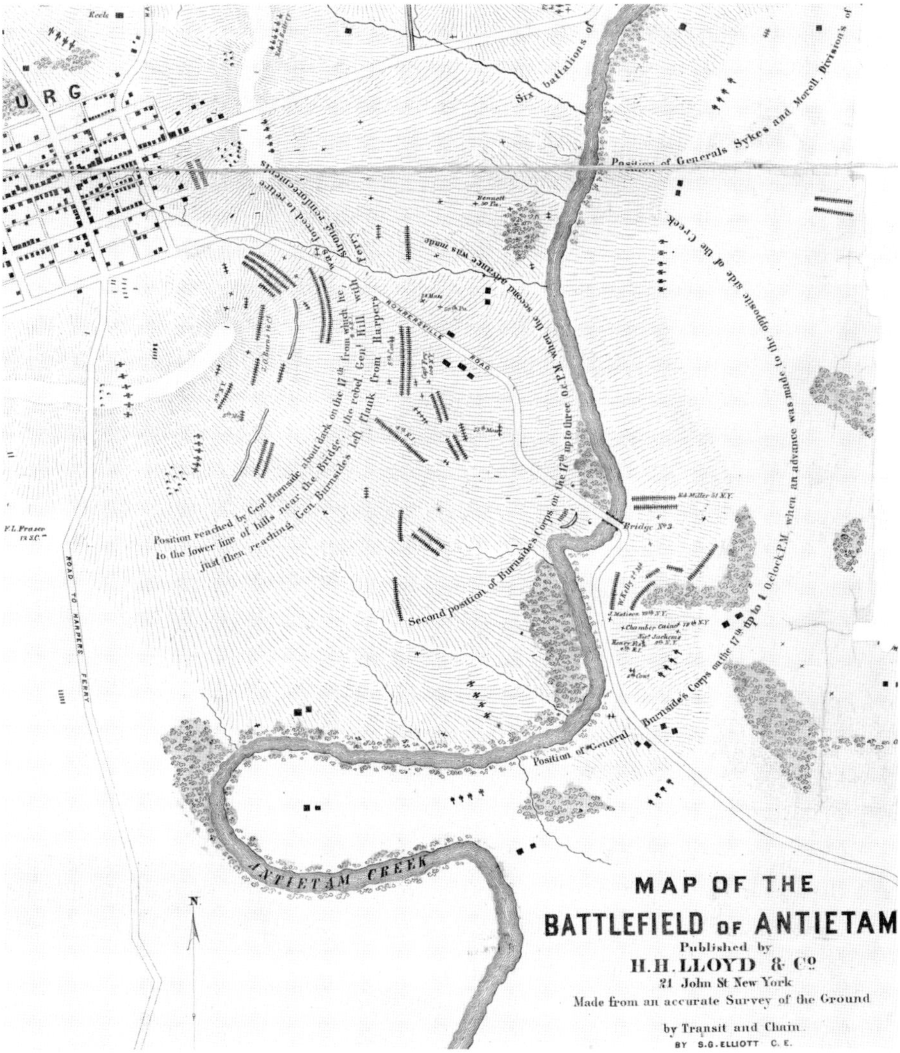

Detail of the Elliot Burial Map. *New York Public Library.*

> *some rebels seemed to have died in the embrace of our own soldiers, and the wounds from shot and shell presented a ghastly sight. Large numbers of soldiers have been detailed to bury all our dead, and it took them two days to do it.*[305]

Losses from this part of the battlefield tell the story of a hard-fought action. In D.R. Jones's division, Kemper's brigade lost 144, Garnett 261 and

Jenkins 235. As a whole, the division suffered 1,435 casualties. A.P. Hill's division only lost 346, half in Gregg's brigade. The total was 63 killed and 283 wounded from Hill's 1,900 soldiers engaged.[306]

Gregg's brigade lost 165 men. The First South Carolina lost 34, Orr's Rifles 12, the Twelfth South Carolina 104 and the Thirteenth 15 men. The Twelfth, which led Gregg's advance into the forty-acre cornfield and was in the center of the line, suffered three times the losses of the next highest unit and nearly ten time the losses of any of the other regiments.[307]

In General James Kemper's brigade of Jones's division, the Seventh Virginia had a mere 113 men and lost 24 killed and wounded with 11 captured. The Seventeenth Virginia lost 35 killed and wounded out of its 46 soldiers. General Robert Toombs's understrength brigade lost 160 of 585 men; the Second Georgia lost 42 of its 97 soldiers. The Fiftieth Georgia, which also assisted in the defense of the creek with Toombs, lost 68 of 250.[308]

Among Union forces, Isaac Rodman's division lost 1,077 of 2,791 engaged, a total of 40 percent and the second highest Union division loss that day. This is a staggering statistic considering how very little attention has been given to this final attack of the day at Antietam. In Harland's brigade, the Sixteenth Connecticut lost a third of their men during their short time in the forty-acre cornfield, 247 of about 700. The Eleventh Connecticut lost 181, and the Eighth Connecticut lost 34 killed and 139 wounded of 400, half their numbers. The Fourth Rhode Island lost a quarter of its men. In all, Harland lost 618 men.[309]

Fairchild's brigade paid heavily for its storied advance that afternoon. The Ninth New York brought 373 men to the fight and lost 54 killed, 158 wounded and 28 missing, a total loss of 240, over half their strength. The Eighty-Ninth New York lost 103 of its 368 men (one third), and the 103rd New York had 117 casualties out of 202 engaged (half of their numbers).[310]

Major Hugh Ewing's brigade of the Kanawha Division was heavily engaged for a brief time near the close of the battle. In that fierce combat at the stone wall, the Twelfth Ohio lost 33 men, the Twenty-Third Ohio lost 69 men and the Thirtieth lost 80.[311]

In their first battle, the Thirty-Fifth Massachusetts lost 69 killed and 150 wounded and missing for a total of 214 out of its 800 men (one fourth). This was the largest loss in Colonel Edward Ferrero's brigade. The Fifty-First New York lost 87 of 335, and the Fifty-First Pennsylvania lost 120 of 335 (one third).[312]

Overall losses were not as high as on other parts of the battlefield, as fewer units were engaged here and the combat was of a shorter duration. Yet some units suffered heavily, and large numbers of dead and wounded were clustered around areas like the Harpers Ferry Road, the forty-acre cornfield, the Rohrbach Bridge and Otto's Lane.

The impact of the battle was devastating for Sharpsburg's families in many ways. Joseph Sherrick owned the forty-acre cornfield and leased it to Leonard Emmert. They intended to split the profits, but the field was "fought over," which damaged the crop, and afterward "the whole field was stripped" for forage for Union horses. Emmert later claimed that he "did not get any of this corn except for a wagon load with husks on." Civilians could file compensation claims after the war for damages to their property but often received a fraction of the estimated value.[313]

John and Katherine Otto's house was occupied as a hospital, and John later claimed that the corn from his barn was consumed by the Union army's animals. His entire supply of wood for the coming winter was used for fuel in the hospital set up in his house. The army occupied the Ottos' "house, barn, beds, furniture &" for seven weeks afterward as a hospital. William Mitchel of the Ninth New York was wounded and taken to the Otto house, where he carved his name into a bedroom window frame. It is visible still.[314]

The armies moved on from Antietam, and the troops gradually rested and recovered. Both forces moved into central Virginia that fall. The Kanawha Division transferred back to West Virginia after Antietam and spent the remainder of the war fighting in that state and the Shenandoah Valley. The Ninth Corps received additional troops by the time of the next major battle at Fredericksburg.[315]

On November 14, new uniforms and blankets arrived from their home state for the South Carolina troops in the Army of Northern Virginia. Thus, before the battle of Fredericksburg, most of the captured Union uniforms from Harpers Ferry would have been shed by Gregg's brigade. Army leaders also feared the confusion that accompanied having so many men in blue in the ranks and ordered the captured unforms replaced.[316]

The veterans of the Sixteenth Connecticut came to a consensus regarding their first fight: they were a new unit and held their ground heroically against long odds. This version of their combat at Antietam was first reported by the *Hartford Evening Press* and became their accepted story, overlooking the rout, terror and confusion of the moment. The article noted that the Confederates called out on them not to fire, were wearing blue uniforms and "treacherously" displayed the United States flag. All the state's units at Antietam performed with "unsullied honor" and displayed "not a symptom of panic," according to the paper. Similarly, the 1889 reunion program from the veterans' visit that year is very matter of fact and does not say that the Sixteenth regiment was routed. This is a natural reaction, as the men had to come to terms with their awful experience.[317]

Many soldiers in their post-battle letters and journals wrote of the Confederates' duplicity in using Union uniforms (verified by numerous accounts) and flags (likely mistaken). Although the Confederates likely used the captured blue coats out of necessity rather than trickery, it helped explain the rout of many troops.

As the War Department preserved the land and placed metal tablets at the park at the close of the nineteenth century, the upper part of the battlefield received greater emphasis. In the area where the Ninth Corps and the divisions of Jones and Hill clashed, only small tracts of land were preserved, linked by an avenue that followed old fencing and farm lanes. This linear feature was where most veterans placed their monuments in these decades. Former soldiers from different states gathered for reunions and monument dedications at different times. In 1903, Ohio dedicated its monuments, followed by Pennsylvania the next year. Connecticut, New York and Massachusetts also placed monuments at different times: the Ninth New York's went up in 1897, for example.

These monuments became not only markers but also statements of pride. The 100th Pennsylvania's veterans were very specific about their monument featuring a young soldier, with the inscription stating that they advanced 195 yards west of that spot, as they couldn't place the monument on the exact spot, which was then private property. Such is the case with other monuments: they could only go where the park owned land, not on the spot where the men fought.[318]

The Ninth New York (Hawkins' Zouaves) monument states that it stands where the unit suffered the greatest loss. They fought in many other engagements, yet the veterans chose Antietam to place their only monument. At the 1897 dedication ceremony, Lillian Elise Horner, daughter of the unit's Major James Horner, wearing a red, white and blue dress, unveiled the monument. Its inscription states that the troops "held it until ordered elsewhere" and "contended with a superior force," both exaggerations, as they were driven back and heavily outnumbered. There are no monuments for their sister regiments, the Eighty-Ninth and 103rd New York.[319]

In the 1890s, the State of Connecticut created a commission to purchase plots of land and design monuments for its regiments at Antietam. It acquired a plot of ground from Mr. Sherrick, a ten-acre portion of the forty-

War Department markers. Directional signs like these line Branch Avenue, indicating the location of various units, since the land was inaccessible in the 1890s. *Author.*

acre cornfield. Called Connecticut Park, it preserved part of the Sixteenth's position but was intended to honor the two other Connecticut regiments that fought nearby. The Eleventh Regiment placed its monument there (which was later moved to a location east of Burnside Bridge to honor their morning attack). Veterans of the Eighth considered putting their monument there as well, but instead, veteran John S. Lane of the regiment purchased a twenty-foot square piece of land to place their regimental monument near where they fought.[320]

In 1937, a National Park Service report recommended acquiring Connecticut Park, noting that there was only a "narrow right of way" from Branch Avenue to the preserved land, "over a long farm lane that is almost impassable."[321]

Thirty-two years after the battle, in 1894, Connecticut dedicated its monuments. Three of the four Connecticut regiments at Antietam were in the Ninth Corps, and the veterans returned to these spots for dedication ceremonies. The events included music, patriotic speeches and poems. The Eighth's monument was veiled before being dedicated, and the Sixteenth's was draped in a flag. It states that this was the unit's "advanced position." The Eighth Connecticut served throughout the war, fighting in many other engagements, but placed only one monument, at Antietam.[322]

The entire group of old soldiers attended each dedication in turn. At the forty-acre cornfield, where the veterans of the Sixteenth regiment placed their monument, Colonel F.W. Cheney spoke. His address was quite short by Victorian standards, and he emphasized that with the regiment's ranks thinning, the monument was important to tell the story of their deeds. "In a few years, only a few of us will be left....Our own work is nearly done. Our children must carry it on." He closed by stating that the spot was "consecrated by the blood of our comrades" and that "here they defended the nation."[323]

Chaplain Charles Dixon spoke of the "noble men whose hearts glowed and burned with patriotic fire" that day. Former surgeon Nathan Mayer also gave a speech. A photo from the dedication shows soldiers and their wives, with a carriage in the background.

The State of Ohio also created a commission to purchase land, design monuments and oversee their placement on the battlefield. Small tracts of land were purchased from farmers for these monuments and the locations marked with wooden boards. Dedicated in 1903, the ceremonies followed the same pattern and formality as those of the other states.[324]

Designed by the commission, the regimental monuments for the Kanawha Division's units are all of similar design: all granite, no metal, no figures or statues, two base styles and similar overall sizes. The Eleventh, Twenty-Eighth and Thirtieth's monuments are all similar, as are the Twenty-Third and Thirty-Sixth's. All prominently feature the word *Ohio* and include carvings of rifles and military gear. The Eleventh's and Twelfth's were placed along Otto Lane, which was not publicly accessible, so small granite directional markers note their location along Branch Avenue. These six regiments who fought throughout the war (Eleventh, Twelfth, Twenty-Third, Twenty-Eighth, Thirtieth and Thirty-Sixth Ohio) placed monuments to their service only here at Antietam.

The Twenty-Third's and Thirtieth's monument positions are important, as they are on the stone wall where they faced Branch's and Archer's brigades. The Thirty-Sixth's monument is near the spot where Colonel Melvin Clarke was killed. Antietam was the only major battle for these Ohio units and their only one with the Army of the Potomac. Having fought in many smaller and lesser-known engagements, they likely wanted to commemorate their actions on the national stage.[325]

This photo from the 1990s shows the Ohio monuments on Branch Avenue. Only a narrow strip of land along the tour route was preserved, the land on either side being private propery. *Author.*

This photo of the same location in 2024 shows the wire fencing removed as the land where the troops maneuvered and fought is now part of the park. *Author.*

Although they did not dedicate monuments at Antietam, Confederate veterans were also active in remembering the war and influenced its commemoration. Postwar memoirs emerged in the 1880s and '90s that fit into the Lost Cause narrative: in this case, outnumbered, hungry, tired Confederates turned back a Union tidal wave. An address of General B.T. Johnson in 1884 noted that at this point in the battle, "the Confederates were used up." Yet the Union had overwhelming numbers at their disposal in the form of three corps: "Franklin was fresh, Porter was fresh, Burnside was fresh….There was no help for Lee unless A.P. Hill got up in time." Of course, the fact is that nearly half of the Ninth Corps had already fought and suffered fatigue and casualties, and the other two corps were not assisting. The Ninth Corps also had many inexperienced troops who were seeing their first combat here.[326]

Veteran David E. Johnston of the Seventh Virginia wrote after the war,

> *In all the battles of the war in which I was engaged—and they were numerous—never did I feel, not even at Gettysburg, so much solicitude for the safety of our army, for I knew that no help could be expected from our left…and there we stood, our division covering nearly a mile of front and numbering not exceeding two thousand muskets, to engage with a force of fifteen thousand well-equipped and well-fed men; while we had little to eat, were almost naked, and many were barefooted.*[327]

Alexander Hunter, a private in the Seventeenth Virginia, wrote after the war of the "dirty, gaunt, tattered" Confederate troops. Their defensive line was a mere "thin string of tattered men, lying there."[328]

David Johnston also wrote that "A.P. Hill, with 2,000 men, assisted by Toombs's Brigade (which at that time didn't number 1,000 present), actually drove back and routed 14,000 fresh Federal soldiers under Burnside, and that, too immediately after a forced march and fording the Potomac!" Veteran Robert T. Mockbee of the Fourteenth Tennessee in Archer's brigade noted that Burnside had fifteen thousand troops, an "overwhelming force," and A.P. Hill had only two thousand men. These outnumbered Southerners "hurled back Burnside's hosts."[329]

This is all not to say that A.P. Hill's attack was insignificant, for it threw the Ninth Corps back and stabilized the Confederate line. Yet it is worthwhile to take the measure of its scale and dig into the details of the attack. There was a good deal of maneuver and back-and-forth by both sides before darkness fell.

Private C.A. Richardson of the Fifteenth Virginia wrote of the "grand exploits of A.P. Hill's 'two thousand men' that memorable September afternoon when the 'dubious tide of battle' hung in the balance ere Burnside was hurled back." All Confederate veterans could agree that the Southerners were outnumbered and still outfought Union troops. Yet there were internal rivalries among some groups.[330]

Conversely, many Union veterans wrote after the war of the overwhelming numbers Hill brought, thus causing the final attack to fail. Lieutenant Henry Brinkerhoff of the Thirtieth Ohio, for example, spoke of Hill's fifteen thousand men, five times the number he actually had.[331]

A major point of contention after the war was the depth of Antietam Creek, which Confederates dismissed as hardly a barrier. Southern veterans described the creek as shallow, making the delays in crossing the creek attributable only to Union incompetence. On the other hand, Union accounts all note that the creek was deep and the banks challenging.[332]

Although not rising to the level of who got the farthest in Pickett's Charge at Gettysburg, there was a postwar controversy arising out of Antietam. Debate ensued among veterans in 1911 about whether McIntosh's Battery was captured or not. This should have been easy to verify, but the debate led to a controversy that endured for several years. The issue prompted an exchange of statements by former Confederate soldiers in *Confederate Veteran Magazine*.

In January 1911, in a short article in *Confederate Veteran Magazine*, Confederate veteran David E. Johnston noted that the Eighth Connecticut overran the battery. In September that year, veteran J.L. Napier of the battery replied with an article claiming that the battery was not captured. He affirmed that the men retired, abandoning the guns and taking the implements so they could neither be fired or spiked. He claims that the Union troops only came within thirty paces of the guns and then were driven back; then the Confederates regained the guns and fired on the retreating enemy. He also noted that the battery's color-bearer captured the lower half of the Eighth's flagstaff and used it for the battery's flag. He claims there were forty-six dead Union soldiers around the fragment of staff.[333]

Johnston replied in the December issue affirming that the battery was captured by the New Englanders, citing reports from A.P. Hill, Longstreet, Jones, Toombs and Burnside. Finally, David G. McIntosh, the battery commander, weighed in the following May, in 1912, a month after the sinking of the *Titanic*. McIntosh said the reports used by Johnston are inaccurate but affirmed that the guns were abandoned in the face of the

Eighth Connecticut's attack, stating it was "better to let the guns go and save the men." Thus he admits their capture: "I always spoke of it as a capture of the battery, and I always gave Toombs' Brigade the credit for the recapture." McIntosh disagrees with Johnston on details, like the capture of a battery flag (which he states they saved and still existed in 1912).[334]

Among Union veterans, a rivalry, not nearly as heated as those about their monuments at Gettysburg, developed about who got the farthest in the final attack of Harland's and Fairchild's units. The men of the Eighth Connecticut, Ninth New York and 100th Pennsylvania claimed the farthest advance.[335]

During the 1894 dedication of the Eighth Connecticut's monument, the unit's chaplain stated, "No regiment of the Ninth Corps advanced so far, or held out so long, or retired in formation so good. By their stubborn fight they saved many others from death or capture." Veterans of the Ninth New York disagreed, citing their own advance. Perhaps because this attack ended in failure, unlike the results of Gettysburg, a great deal of time was not spent debating it. Veterans of the two Fifty-Firsts, from New York and Pennsylvania, disagree over who made it first over the Rohrbach bridge but this did not develop into a major controversy.[336]

Some Union veterans also argued about making it into the village of Sharpsburg. A Pennsylvania veteran wrote just a month after the battle,

> *The 45th was the only regiment that entered Sharpsburg, driving the rebels through the town. Not another regiment approached within 300 yards of the town. There is no telling where we would have halted had not our old Colonel recalled us.... We claim no special credit for all this—we simply did our duty.*

He went on to write, "Had a New York regiment performed the same feat," it would have been more publicized.[337]

After the more complete preservation and interpretation of this sector of the battlefield in the 2000s, historians and visitors can now turn their attention to details previously inaccessible to them. Otto Lane provides one of best views of any part of the Antietam battlefield. Here one can see nearly all key areas of this part of the field. Until 2006, visitors to the park could not take in this important view.

At the lower part of the battlefield, Confederates effectively used artillery, perhaps just as well or better than anywhere else on September 17. Ninth Corps accounts noted the consistent and intense incoming fire from start to finish that day. When Cox launched the final attack at three o'clock in the afternoon, the Confederates had an artillery advantage, which only grew as Hill's division arrived.[338]

A great deal of maneuver and fighting happened in an area that was not very large, bounded by the Boonsboro Pike, Harpers Ferry Road and the creek. The action began with three assaults on the bridge and then a general movement forward toward town; the attack by Fairchild's brigade; the Eighth Connecticut's charge; the Confederate counterattack at the forty-acre cornfield; the counterattack of Toombs, Archer, and Branch; and, finally, Ewing's advance to and fighting along the stone wall (now Branch Avenue).

The preservation and interpretation of this area has undergone many changes. Antietam is one of the oldest battlefield parks, first preserved in 1890 by the War Department and later by the National Park Service. Evidence of early preservation and commemoration is seen in the monuments, plaques, avenues and reconstructed stone walls in this area. For the most part, these later features do not impact the integrity of the 1862 landscape.

Early preservation at Antietam focused on key areas such as the Cornfield, the Sunken Road and Burnside's Bridge. For the most part, avenues of land, often following farm lanes, were purchased for a tour route through the rural landscape. In time, more of the upper battlefield was preserved. In the lower area, much of the land was not accessible to visitors or historians. This gradually changed in the early twenty-first century. Until 2006, for example, the Eleventh Ohio, Twelfth Ohio and Sixteenth Connecticut's monuments were not accessible to the public.

The orientation film shown in the visitor center for decades, *Antietam Visit*, dramatized the attacks on the Rohrbach bridge and gave the impression that the battle was over once it was carried. On the battlefield driving tour, the final leg of the drive along Branch Avenue did not allow for widespread exploration, and it was difficult to stop anywhere along the route, forcing visitors to ride along the battle line with little in the way of narrative due to the small amount of land available to the park.

In 1992, the park created a general management plan, which prioritized the restoration of the historic landscape. With new land acquisition, the park could also interpret areas that had never been open to visitors. The plan states,

> *The battlefield offers a unique opportunity to accomplish this goal because the landscape within and surrounding it has remained largely rural and agricultural since that time. Today visitors are asked to use their imagination*

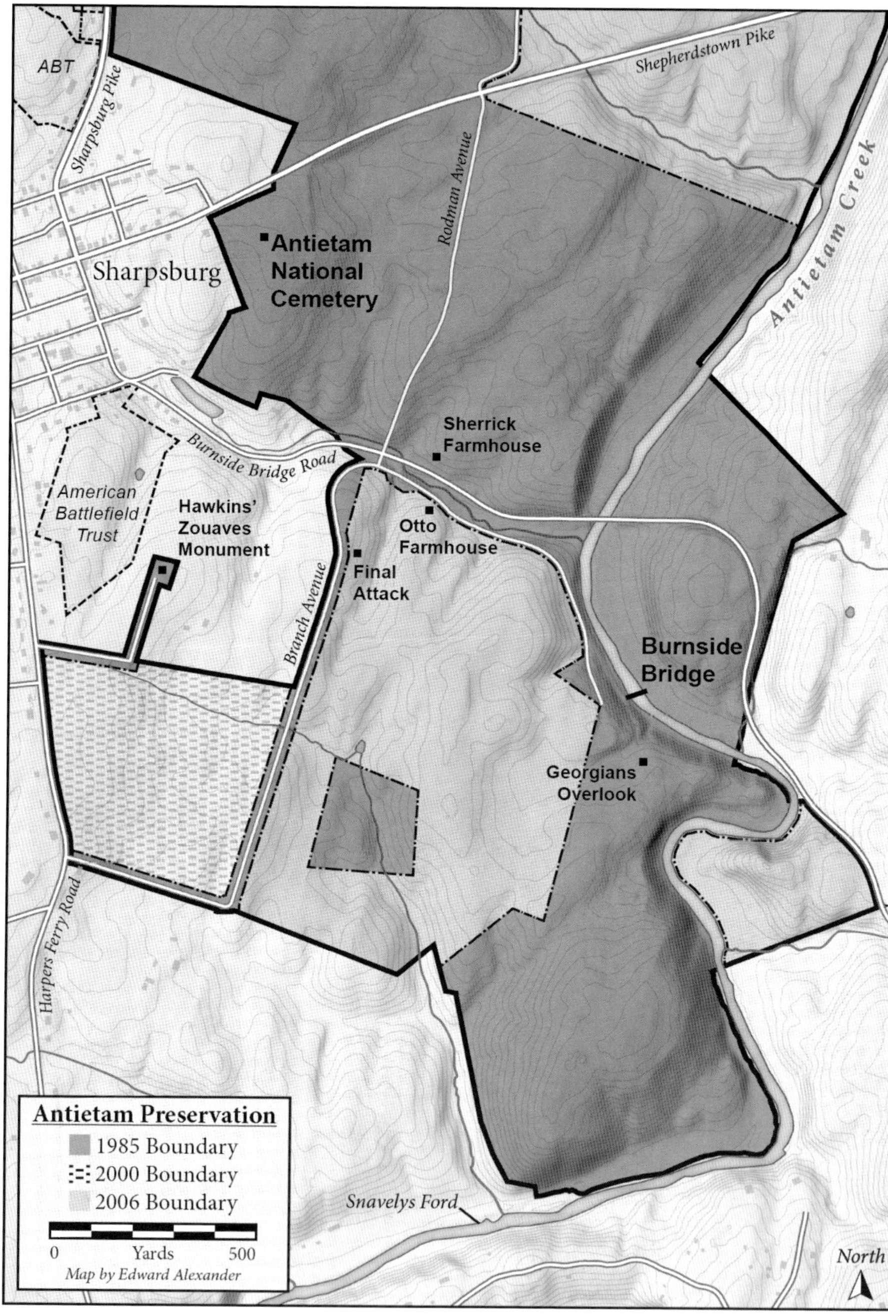

Preservation of the lower part of the battlefield. *Edward Alexander.*

in understanding the actions that took place during the day-long battle. Scene restoration—restoring historic trace roads, farmhouses, and farm fields, replacing fence lines, and reestablishing woods and orchards—would help them to better visualize and appreciate this tragic event.[339]

In 1996, Antietam National Battlefield complemented an innovative interpretive plan with the goal of providing access and interpretation to the new land by focusing on appreciation of the landscape and terrain. The park created a series of Discovery Trails, providing in-depth explorations of key areas of the battlefield while remaining sensitive to the landscape. The trails were designed to blend harmoniously with the terrain, often using just a mowed path, and focused on fields of view and providing access to key areas of combat. The park added two of these new trails to the lower battlefield: the Burnside's Bridge and Final Attack Trails. Quoting from the interpretive plan: "Each trail head will have small, low profile, trailhead waysides (signs)," and signage on the trails would be minimal. The trails were designed to "lay lightly on the land."[340]

One of the Discovery Trails that takes visitors into the landscape to better understand the battle and appreciate the terrain. *Author.*

A sign at the intersection of two trails near the forty-acre cornfield (*in the background*). This key part of the battlefield may now be explored. *Author.*

The Discovery Trails emphasized themes such as the importance of topography in defining the "nature, tactics, and flow of battle" and the important role of artillery. They also, for the first time, allowed access to areas never before seen by the public, such as Otto's Lane, the forty-acre cornfield and various monuments like those of the Sixteenth Connecticut and Twelfth Ohio. Further plans for new trails will take visitors into land acquired since the first planning documents of the 1990s and give visitors more exploration options. Now the battlefield known for having one of the most pristine Civil War period landscapes has public access to explore, appreciate and study the battle in that landscape.[341]

The last act of the battle of Antietam that September afternoon was a confusing, chaotic and complicated action. With more complete preservation of the site by the 2000s and improved access with trails and markers, it is now possible to fully appreciate the actions here. An entire section of the battlefield, once neglected by photographers, early preservationists and historians, is now able to be fully interpreted and appreciated. This part of the battlefield holds stories of fighting, maneuver, triumph and tragedy worth exploring.

ORDER OF BATTLE

United States Forces

Ninth Army Corps
Major General Ambrose Burnside
Major General Jacob D. Cox

First Division
Brigadier General Orlando B. Willcox

First Brigade
Colonel Benjamin Christ
Twenty-Eighth Massachusetts
Seventeenth Michigan
Seventy-Ninth New York
Fiftieth Pennsylvania

Second Brigade
Colonel Thomas Welsh
Eighth Michigan
Forty-Sixth New York
Forty-Fifth Pennsylvania
100th Pennsylvania
Massachusetts Light, Eighth Battery
Second U.S., Battery E

Second Division
Brigadier General Samuel D. Sturgis

First Brigade
Brigadier General James Nagle
Second Maryland
Sixth New Hampshire
Ninth New Hampshire
Forty-Eighth Pennsylvania

Second Brigade
Colonel Edward Ferrero
Twenty-First Massachusetts
Thirty-Fifth Massachusetts
Fifty-First New York
Fifty-First Pennsylvania
Pennsylvania Light Artillery, Battery D
Fourth U.S., Battery E

Third Division
Brigadier General Isaac Rodman

First Brigade
Colonel Harrison Fairchild
Ninth New York
Eighty-Ninth New York
103rd New York

Second Brigade
Colonel Edward Harland
Eighth Connecticut
Eleventh Connecticut
Sixteenth Connecticut
Fourth Rhode Island
Fifth U.S., Battery A Ninth New York, Company K

Kanawha Division
Colonel Eliakim P. Scammon

First Brigade
Colonel Hugh Ewing
Twelfth Ohio
Twenty-Third Ohio
Thirtieth Ohio
First Ohio Light, Battery L

Second Brigade
Colonel George Crook
Eleventh Ohio
Twenty-Eighth Ohio
Thirty-Sixth Ohio
Kentucky Light Artillery

Confederate Forces

Jones's Division
Brigadier General David R. Jones

Toombs's Brigade
Brigadier General Robert Toombs
Second Georgia
Fifteenth Georgia
Seventeenth Georgia
Twentieth Georgia

Drayton's Brigade
Brigadier Gen Thomas Drayton
Fiftieth Georgia
Fifty-First Georgia
Fifteenth South Carolina
Third South Carolina Battalion

Garnett's Brigade
Brigadier General Richard Garnett
Eighth Virginia
Eighteenth Virginia
Nineteenth Virginia
Twenty-Eighth Virginia
Fifty-Sixth Virginia

Jenkins's Brigade
Colonel Joseph Walker
First South Carolina Volunteers
Second South Carolina Rifles
Fifth South Carolina
Sixth South Carolina
Fourth South Carolina Battalion
Palmetto Sharpshooters

KEMPER'S BRIGADE
Brigadier General James Kemper
First Virginia
Seventh Virginia
Eleventh Virginia
Seventeenth Virginia
Twenty-Fourth Virginia
Wise's Battery (Virginia)

A.P. HILL'S DIVISION
Major General Ambrose P. Hill

BRANCH'S BRIGADE
Brigadier General Lawrence O. Branch
Seventh North Carolina
Twenty-Eighth North Carolina
Thirty-Third North Carolina
Thirty-Seventh North Carolina

GREGG'S BRIGADE
Brigadier General Maxcey Gregg
First South Carolina Provisional
Twelfth South Carolina
Thirteenth South Carolina
Fourteenth South Carolina
First South Carolina Rifles

ARCHER'S BRIGADE
Brigadier General James J. Archer
Nineteenth Georgia
First Tennessee
Seventh Tennessee
Fourteenth Tennessee

ARTILLERY BATTALION, REUBEN L. WALKER
Fredericksburg Battery (Virginia)
Pee Dee Battery (South Carolina)
Purcell Battery (Virginia)
Crenshaw's Battery (Virginia)

NOTES

Introduction

1. Frassanitto, *Antietam*, 244.
2. Kolakowski, "Success and Failure," 1.
3. Liska and Perlotto, *Eighth Connecticut Volunteer Infantry*, 73.
4. Hartwig, *To Antietam Creek*, 141, 492, 591; Greene, "Fought the Battle Splendidly," 67; Murfin, *Gleam of Bayonets*, 276–78; Sears, *Landscape Turned Red*, 170–71. Every historian of the Antietam Campaign has debated the intention of the wing system and its abrupt end, each offering their interpretations. It is an important aspect of understanding the battle and may likely never be resolved.
5. Marvel, *Burnside*, 129.
6. Cox, "Battle of Antietam."
7. *Final Attack Trail*, 1.

Chapter 1

8. Hartwig, *I Dread the Thought.*
9. Kolakowski, "Success and Failure," 19.
10. Hardy, *General Lee's Immortals*, 101; Clary, *15th South Carolina Infantry*, 62; *War of the Rebellion* (hereafter cited as O.R.) 19, part 1, 866.
11. Clary, *15th South Carolina Infantry*, 68.
12. Marvel, *Burnside*, 134; Benning, "Notes," 393; O.R. supplement, 889.

13. Dameron, *Benning's Brigade*, 22.
14. Dameron, *Benning's Brigade*, 23; McRae, "Benning's Brigade."
15. Dameron, *Benning's Brigade*, 24; Fogle, letter to Dr. J. Fogle; O.R. 19, part 1, 573.
16. McRae, "Benning's Brigade"; Lokey, *My Experiences*, 10.
17. *Final Attack Trail*; Johnson and Anderson, *Artillery Hell*, 88, 90.
18. K.M. Walker, *Antietam Farmsteads*, 100–07.
19. K.M. Walker, *Antietam Farmsteads*, 102; Lokey, *My Experiences*, 10.
20. Hudson, letter to Sophy Hudson.
21. Greene, "Fought the Battle Splendidly," 73; Marvel, *Burnside*, 140; Kolakowski, "Success and Failure," 19; O.R. 19, part 2, 307.
22. O.R. 19, part 2, 314; Cox, *Reminiscences*, 304; Kolakowski, "Success and Failure," 19; Marvell, *Burnside*, 5, 6, 9, 11. Duane served with distinction as chief engineer with the Army of the Potomac through its later campaigns, and perhaps his finest accomplishment was the construction of a two-thousand-foot-long pontoon bridge over the James River in 1864 as the army advanced on Petersburg, the longest pontoon bridge built during the war. Yet his performance here was less than stellar. He and Burnside crossed paths again in 1864 outside of Petersburg when troops from the Ninth Corps proposed tunneling under Confederate defenses. Duane was skeptical of the plan, spoke against it and, after General Grant's approval, did little to support the effort. The resulting battle of the Crater doomed Burnside's career.
23. Todd, *Seventy-Ninth New York Volunteers*, 237; Blakeslee, "Sixteenth at Antietam," 14–16.
24. *Thirty-Fifth Massachusetts Volunteers*, 45.
25. O.R. 19, part 2, 424, 429.
26. Cox, "Battle of Antietam," 633, 650; Cox, *Reminiscences*, 333, 341.
27. O.R. 19, part 1, 844; Greene, "Fought the Battle Splendidly," 73–77.
28. Murfin, *Gleam of Bayonets*, 241, 273; O.R. 19, part 1, 419, 444, 452; Cox, *Reminiscences*, 334.
29. O.R. 19, part 1, 914; Cox, "Battle of Antietam," 651; J.G. Walker, "Sharpsburg," 676.
30. *Union Advance Trail*, 10; Schildt, *Ninth Corps at Antietam*, 103.
31. *Union Advance Trail*, 10; Tillinghart, "Fighting Them Over."
32. Sears, *Landscape Turned Red*, 262–63; *Souvenir of Excursion*, 37–38; *Union Assault Trail*, 10.
33. Pawlak and Welch, *Ohio at Antietam*, 68–69, 92.
34. Cunningham and Miller, *Antietam*, 55, 57.

35. Cox, *Reminiscences*, 340, 343.
36. Jackman, *Sixth New Hampshire Regiment*, 54–55.
37. Dimon, "Federal Surgeon at Sharpsburg," 142; O.R. 19, part 1, 197.
38. Dimon, "Federal Surgeon at Sharpsburg," 141.
39. O.R. 19, part 1, 447; Priest, *George Wren's Diary*, 71.
40. Priest, *George Wren's Diary*, 73.
41. "Burke Sharpshooters," 464; Fogle, letter to Dr. J. Fogle.
42. O.R. 19, part 1, 890.
43. Lord, *Ninth New Hampshire Volunteers*, 125; Murfin, *Gleam of Bayonets*, 274.
44. Cox, *Reminiscences*, 343; Murfin, *Gleam of Bayonets*, 274.
45. Pawlak, "Bridge for Whiskey." Parker stated that a ration of two to four ounces of "quinine and whiskey had to be resorted to prevent fever and ague, and other diseases incident to a marshy country."
46. Pawlak, "Bridge for Whiskey."
47. Cox, *Reminiscences*, 343.
48. Parker, *51st Regiment*, 232; Pawlak, "Bridge for Whiskey."
49. Bolton, War Diary.
50. Pawlak, "Bridge for Whiskey."
51. Parker, *51st Regiment*, 234; Murfin *Gleam of Bayonets*, 275.
52. Parker, *51st Regiment*, 234.
53. Fogle, letter to Dr. J. Fogle.
54. Benning, "Notes," 393.
55. Dameron, *Benning's Brigade*, 24; "Burke Sharpshooters."
56. "Fiftieth Georgia Regiment," *Savannah Republican*.
57. Dameron, *Benning's Brigade*, 25; Fogle, letter to Dr. J. Fogle.
58. Fogle, letter to Dr. J. Fogle; Carman, *Maryland Campaign*, 424. W.S. Shepherd of the Second Georgia stated that his regiment rallied in this cornfield.
59. O.R. 19, part 1, 891; Dameron, *Benning's Brigade*, 25; Dugan, letter to the *Central Georgian*; Benning, "Notes," 394.
60. Murfin, *Gleam of Bayonets*, 275.
61. Parker, *51st Regiment*, 235–36.
62. Dimon, "Federal Surgeon at Sharpsburg," 144.
63. Dimon, "Federal Surgeon at Sharpsburg," 144; Walcott, *21st Regiment Massachusetts Volunteers*, 200–01.
64. *Thirty-Fifth Massachusetts*, 41–42.
65. *Thirty-Fifth Massachusetts*, 42–43.
66. *Thirty-Fifth Massachusetts*, 44–45.
67. Graham, *Ninth Regiment, New York Volunteers*, 57–58; Lord, *Ninth New Hampshire Volunteers*, 105–6, 129.

68. Lord, *Ninth New Hampshire Volunteers*, 125.
69. Lord, *Ninth New Hampshire Volunteers*, 126.
70. O.R. 19, part 1, 449. It is unclear if Burnside or Cox felt that timing was critical since they may have been under the impression that they were to merely create a diversion in favor of the main attack to the north.
71. Parker, *51st Regiment*, 238.
72. Cox, *Reminiscences*, 344.
73. Bosbyshell, *48th in the War*, 81–82.
74. Priest, *George Wren's Diary*, 72–73.
75. Bosbyshell, *48th in the War*, 80.
76. Gould, *Story of the 48th*, 89.
77. Gould, *Story of the 48th*, 91; Johnson and Anderson, *Artillery Hell*, 77–78.
78. Bosbyshell, *48th in the War*, 80.
79. Cox, "Battle of Antietam," 651, 653; O.R. 19, part 1, 425.
80. Carman, *Maryland Campaign*, 431; Cox, "Battle of Antietam," 653; Cox, *Reminiscences*, 345.
81. Graham, *Ninth Regiment, New York Volunteers*, 299.
82. Parker, *51st Regiment*, 239–40.
83. Jackman, *Sixth New Hampshire Regiment*, 108–09.
84. Todd, *Seventy-Ninth New York Volunteers*, 242–43.
85. "Letter from 51st Penna," *National Defender*.
86. Schmitt, *General George Crook*, 98; Gottfried, *Maps of Antietam*, 215.
87. Hudson, letter to Sophy Hudson.

Chapter 2

88. Graham, *Ninth Regiment, New York Volunteers*, 289; Brinkerhoff, *Thirtieth Regiment Ohio Volunteer Infantry*, 45; Merriman, letter to Merriman.
89. Johnson, *Long Roll*, 191.
90. Williams, "Rodman's Brigade at Antietam"; Graham, *Ninth Regiment, New York Volunteers*, 289; Thompson, "With Burnside at Antietam," 661.
91. Johnson, *Long Roll*, 191.
92. Graham, *Ninth Regiment, New York Volunteers*, 282; Todd, *Seventy-Ninth New York Volunteers*, 237.
93. Johnson, *Long Roll*, 188; Spooner, "Maryland Campaign," 229–30; Liska and Perlotto, *Eighth Connecticut Volunteer Infantry*, 73.

94. Gordon, *Broken Regiment*, 31; Kellogg, Diary; Merriman, letter to Merriman; *Souvenir of Excursion*, 16; Cunningham and Miller, *Antietam*, 77; Thompson, "With Burnside at Antietam," 661; Graham, letter to Hawkins, 4.
95. Spooner, "Maryland Campaign," 229–30; Allen, *Forty-Six Months*, 143; *Souvenir of Excursion*, 17–18; Gordon, *Broken Regiment*, 31.
96. Allen, *Forty-Six Months*, 143.
97. Whitney, *Hawkins Zouaves*; Graham, letter to Hawkins, 4.
98. Carman, *Maryland Campaign*, 427; Pawlak, email to author, February 21, 2022; Clemmens, email to author.
99. Compton, *Autobiography*, 103.
100. Pawlak and Welch, *Ohio at Antietam*, 79.
101. Blakeslee, *Sixteenth Connecticut Volunteers*, 15.
102. Thompson, "With Burnside at Antietam," 661.
103. Graham, letter to Hawkins, 5.
104. Whitney, *Hawkins Zouaves*, 141; Johnson and Anderson, *Artillery Hell*, 78; Liska and Perlotto, *Eighth Connecticut Volunteer Infantry*, 77; Carman, *Maryland Campaign*, 430–32.
105. Graham, *Ninth Regiment, New York Volunteers*, 291–92.
106. Tillinghart, "Fighting Them Over."
107. Whitney, *Hawkins Zouaves*, 142–43.
108. Hartwig, *I Dread the Thought*, 524; Hardy, *Lee's Immortals*, 102; Clark, *Histories*, 33; *Recollections and Reminiscences* 5:512.
109. Hudson, letter to Hudson.

Chapter 3

110. Clary, *15th South Carolina Infantry*, 64.
111. Cox, "Battle of Antietam," 655; Cox, *Reminiscences*, 346–47.
112. O.R. 19, part 1, 438–39.
113. Unidentified newspaper article, 50th Pennsylvania Regimental File, Antietam National Battlefield.
114. K.M. Walker, *Antietam Farmsteads*, 88–96.
115. O.R. 19, part 1, 898–900; Cox, "Battle of Antietam," 655; Cox, *Reminiscences*, 347.
116. Horton and Terebaugh, *Eleventh Regiment Ohio Volunteer Infantry*, 75.
117. Baldwin, *Struck Eagle*, 170–71; O.R. 19, part 1, 907–08.
118. Mixson, *Reminiscences of a Private*, 29–31.

119. *Voices of the Civil War*, 125–26.
120. O.R. 19, part 1, 431; Mixson, *Reminiscences of a Private*, 32.
121. Mixson, *Reminiscences of a Private*, 32–34.
122. K.M. Walker, *Antietam Farmsteads*, 93.
123. Gavin, *Campaigning with the Roundheads*, 166; O.R. 19 part 1, 430.
124. Gavin, *Campaigning with the Roundheads*, 170.
125. Gavin, *Campaigning with the Roundheads*, 174; Greene, *Infantryman Pettit*, 11.
126. Gavin, *Campaigning with the Roundheads*, 167; O.R. 19, 441.
127. Gavin, *Campaigning with the Roundheads*, 69; O.R. 19, 442.
128. Carman, *Maryland Campaign*, 443; "Our Army Correspondence," *Columbia Spy*.
129. Carman, *Maryland Campaign*, 443; Baldwin, *Struck Eagle*, 17; Hartwig, *I Dread the Thought*, 554.
130. Albert, *Forty-Fifth Regiment*, 49; Jones, "General B.T. Johnson," 532–33; Clary, *15th South Carolina Infantry*, 67.
131. Johnson, *Long Roll*, 144; Carman, *Maryland Campaign*, 436, 456.
132. Johnson, *Long Roll*, 28; Wallace, *17th Virginia Infantry*, 40; Hunter, "High Private's Sketch," 18.
133. Durkin, *John Dooley*, 45.
134. Clary, *15th South Carolina Infantry*, 66; O.R. 19, part 1, 451.
135. Johnston, "Battle of Sharpsburg," 28.
136. Durkin, *John Dooley*, 47.
137. Bell, *11th Virginia Infantry*, 33; O.R. 19, part 1, 891, 910, 912.
138. Riggs, *Seventh Virginia Infantry*, 16; Johnston, "Battle of Sharpsburg," 145.
139. Durkin, *John Dooley*, 46; Hunter, "High Private's Sketch," 18.
140. Johnston, "Battle of Sharpsburg," 28.
141. Hunter, "High Private's Sketch," 17–18.
142. Hunter, "High Private's Sketch," 18; *Voices of the Civil War*, 127; Brock, "Battle of Antietam," 42–43.
143. Wallace, *17th Virginia*, 120; Hunter, "High Private's Sketch," 16.
144. Hunter, "High Private's Sketch," 16.
145. Pawlak, email to author, June 22, 2024.
146. Evans, *Confederate Military History*, 129.
147. Clark, *Histories*, 1:574–75. There were no Virginians among Hill's first arriving units; perhaps their flag was mistaken for a Virginia state flag.
148. Carman, *Maryland Campaign*, 456, 463; Pawlak, email to author, June 22, 2024; Pendleton, letter, September 22, 1862; O.R. 19, part 1, 164.
149. Cox, *Reminiscences*, 348.

Chapter 4

150. O.R. 19, part 1, 984; Johnson and Anderson, *Artillery Hell*, 52, 93–94; Jones and Evans, *Treasured Reminiscences*, 43; Brunson, *Pee Dee Light Artillery*, 20.
151. McIntosh, "McIntosh's Battery at Sharpsburg," 204.
152. *Recollections and Reminiscences*, 5:506.
153. Brunson, *Pee Dee Light Artillery*, 6, 21; O.R. 19, part 1, 981.
154. Hartwig, *I Dread the Thought*, 509.
155. Johnston, "Battle of Sharpsburg," 28; Johnston, *Confederate Boy*, 145; Dugan, letter to the *Central Georgian*, 101.
156. Graham, letter to Hawkins, 6.
157. Whitney, *Hawkins Zouaves*, 143–48.
158. Graham, *Ninth Regiment*, 296–97.
159. Lord, *Ninth New Hampshire Volunteers*, 129; Longacre, *Antietam to Fort Fisher*, 38–39.
160. "Colors of the Ninth Regiment."
161. "Fighting Them Over," 4; Whitney, *Hawkins Zouaves*, 149.
162. Unknown letter, Ninth New York Regimental File, Antietam National Battlefield.
163. Thompson, "With Burnside at Antietam," 661.
164. Hine, Diary.
165. Johnson, *Long Roll*, 192.
166. *Thirty-Fifth Massachusetts*, 45.
167. Thompson, "With Burnside at Antietam," 660–62.
168. *Voices of the Civil War*, 127–28; Graham, *Ninth Regiment*, 293–96.
169. New York State Military Museum and Veterans Research Center, "9th New York Infantry."
170. Johnson, *Long Roll*, 189.
171. Graham, *Ninth Regiment*, 297, 318.
172. O.R. 19, part 1, 451.
173. Johnson, *Long Roll*, 192–94.
174. Graham, *Ninth Regiment*, 303–08, 318, 313.
175. Johnson, *Long Roll*, 194–95.
176. O.R. 19: part 1, 431; Graham, *Ninth Regiment*, 303; Cox, "Battle of Antietam," 655.
177. O.R. 19: part 1, 892, 904; Wallace, *17th Virginia*, 40, 41; Johnston, "Battle of Antietam," 28; Johnston, *Confederate Boy*, 145; Whisterer, *New York*, 127.
178. Almon, letter to parents.

179. Hunter, "High Private's Sketch," 18; *Voices of the Civil War*, 127; Brock, "Battle of Antietam," 42–43.
180. Hine, Diary; *Thirty-Fifth Massachusetts*, 46.
181. *Thirty-Fifth Massachusetts*, 47.
182. *Thirty-Fifth Massachusetts*, 47.
183. Brock, "Battle of Antietam," 42.
184. *Thirty-Fifth Massachusetts*, 48, 50.
185. "Fiftieth Georgia Regiment," *Savannah Republican*; *Recollections and Reminiscences*, 5:506.
186. Liska and Perlotto, *Eighth Connecticut Volunteer Infantry*, 79, 73.
187. Carman, *Maryland Campaign*, 459; Liska and Perlotto, *Eighth Connecticut Volunteer Infantry*, 81.
188. Benning, "Notes," 394; O.R. 19, part 1, 573; O.R. supplement, 164; Carman, *Maryland Campaign*, 460.
189. Liska and Perlotto, *Eighth Connecticut Volunteer Infantry*, 81–82.
190. Marsh, letter to Marsh.
191. Liska and Perlotto, *Eighth Connecticut Volunteer Infantry*, 83.
192. Johnston, "Battle of Antietam," 28; Tillinghart, "Fighting Them Over."
193. Hardy, *Thirty-Seventh North Carolina Troops*, 100; Blakeslee, *Sixteenth Connecticut Volunteers*, 16.
194. Gottfried, *Maps of Antietam*, 297; O.R. 19, part 1, 426; Spooner, "Maryland Campaign," 235; Liska and Perlotto, *Eighth Connecticut Volunteer Infantry*, 83. The marker says Rodman was hit 265 yards to the south; that spot would be in the ravine behind the Eighth Connecticut's position.
195. Liska and Perlotto, *Eighth Connecticut Volunteer Infantry*, 83.
196. Clary, *15th South Carolina Infantry*, 86; Clark, *Histories*, 1:372, 2:71.
197. Jordan, *North Carolina Troops*, 32–33.
198. Hardy, *Thirty-Seventh*, 103.
199. Liska and Perlotto, *Eighth Connecticut Volunteer Infantry*, 83; "Fiftieth Georgia Regiment," *Savannah Republican*.
200. Lokey, *My Experiences*, 12; Dugan, letter to the *Central Georgian*, 101–02; Carman, *Maryland Campaign*, 548.
201. Lokey, *My Experiences*, 12.
202. Hardy, *Thirty-Seventh*, 103.
203. Hardy, *Thirty-Seventh*, 103–04; Clark, *Histories*, 2:32–33, 656.
204. Marsh, letter to Marsh.
205. O.R. 19, part 1, 1000–01.
206. Mockbee, *14th Tennessee Regiment of Infantry*.
207. Gottfried, *Maps of Antietam*, 297.

208. Motlow, "Campaigns in Northern Virginia," 310; Gottfried, *Maps of Antietam*, 297.
209. Lord, *Ninth New Hampshire Volunteers*, 61–62; 118.
210. Croffut and Morris, *Military and Cultural History*, 272–73; *Souvenir of Excursion*, 25; O.R. 19, part 1, 455.
211. Croffut and Morris, *Military and Cultural History*, 276.
212. Hardy, *Thirty-Seventh*, 100.
213. O.R. 19, part 1, 887; Dugan, letter to the *Central Georgian*, 101.
214. Johnston, "Battle of Antietam," 29.

Chapter 5

215. Cunningham and Miller, *Antietam*, 25–26; Armstrong, *Major McKinley*, 39.
216. Pawlak and Welch, *Ohio at Antietam*, 79–80; Compton, *Autobiography*, 103.
217. Brinkerhoff, *Thirtieth Regiment Ohio Volunteer Infantry*, 45.
218. Walton, "30th Ohio."
219. O.R. 19, part 1, 470; Cunningham and Miller, *Antietam*, 78.
220. Walton, "30th Ohio."
221. Brinkerhoff, *Thirtieth Regiment Ohio Volunteer Infantry*, 45, 47.
222. Hardy, *Thirty-Seventh*, 103.
223. Pawlak and Welch, *Ohio at Antietam*, 83; Adams, *Monuments at Antietam*, 62–63; Watts, letter to *Plain Dealer*.
224. O.R. 19, part 1, 468.
225. Hardy, *Thirty-Seventh*, 100; Carman, *Maryland Campaign*, 475.
226. Brinkerhoff, *Thirtieth Regiment Ohio Volunteer Infantry*, 46.
227. Pawlak and Welch, *Ohio at Antietam*, 83; Adams, *Monuments at Antietam*, 62; Watts, letter to *Plain Dealer*.
228. *Final Attack Trail*, 9; Johnson and Anderson, *Artillery Hell*, 78.
229. Adams, *Monuments at Antietam*, 62–63; Compton, *Autobiography*, 103; O.R. 19, part 1, 466; Carman, *Maryland Campaign*, 482.
230. Adams, *Monuments at Antietam*, 57.
231. Adams, *Monuments at Antietam*, 90–91; Schmitt, *General George Crook*, 99.
232. Schmitt, *General George Crook*, 99.
233. Adams, *Monuments at Antietam*, 91.
234. Schmitt, *General George Crook*, 100; Adams, *Monuments at Antietam*, 70, 78.

235. Pawlak and Welch, *Ohio at Antietam*, 85; O.R. 19, part 1, 467, 478; Adams, *Monuments at Antietam*, 78; Cox, *Reminiscences*, 348.
236. Hardy, *Thirty-Seventh*, 100.

Chapter 6

237. Johnson and Anderson, *Artillery Hell*, 52; Rosebrock, "A.P. Hill or Artillery." Rosebrock points out several factors that gave the Confederates an edge in artillery, including the bottleneck at the bridge for Union reinforcements, limited room for deployment and low ammunition by the afternoon.
238. O.R. 19, part 1, 981.
239. Pawlak, email to author, February 21, 2022; Pendleton letter.
240. Wardlow, Diary; Pawlak, email to author, June 22, 2024.
241. Pawlak, email to author, June 22, 2024; Pendleton letter; O.R. 19, part 1, 988.
242. Caldwell, *Brigade of South Carolinians*, 75; Brock, "Lieutenant General A.P. Hill," 181.
243. O.R. 19, part 1, 985–86; Evans, *Confederate Military History*, 129.
244. Sears, *Landscape Turned Red*, 288; Cowie, *Hell Came to Sharpsburg*, 75.
245. *Excursion and Reunion*, 18–19.
246. Corffut and Morris, *Military and Cultural History*, 270–71; O.R. 19 part 1, 453. Burnside received the news from the signal station on Elk Mountain and relayed it, but the officers at the front discovered it for themselves.
247. *Excursion and Reunion*, 19; Cox, *Reminiscences*, 348; Blakeslee, "Sixteenth at Antietam;" 14–16; Gordon, *Broken Regiment*, 32–33.
248. *Excursion and Reunion*, 7.
249. Blakeslee, "Sixteenth at Antietam," 14–16.
250. O.R. 19, part 1, 989; Carman, *Maryland Campaign*, 465, 461; Caldwell, *Brigade of South Carolinians*, 45, 76; *Recollections and Reminiscences*, 5:461.
251. O.R. 19, part 1, 999; Wardlow, Diary; Carman, *Maryland Campaign*, 265; Hardy, *Thirty-Seventh*, 100; Caldwell, *Brigade of South Carolinians*, 77–78.
252. O.R. 19, part 1, 992.
253. O.R. 19, part 1, 994.
254. Caldwell, *Brigade of South Carolinians*, 45–46; O.R. 19, part 1, 997; Daly, *Alexander Cheves Haskell*, 81.
255. Daly, *Alexander Cheves Haskell*, 81; O.R. 19, part 1, 981.
256. Caldwell, *Brigade of South Carolinians*, 76–77.
257. Croffut and Morris, *Military and Cultural History*, 271.

258. Blakeslee, "Sixteenth at Antietam," 14–16; Burnham, to mother and family, October 4, 1862.
259. Arnold, "At Antietam"; Blakeslee, "Sixteenth at Antietam," 14–16.
260. Arnold, "At Antietam."
261. *Excursion and Reunion*, 20.
262. Kellogg, Diary.
263. Blakeslee, *Sixteenth Connecticut Volunteers*, 16, 102; Priest, *16th Connecticut Volunteer Infantry*, 26.
264. Bauer, letter to Bauer.
265. Cuzner, letter to Van Dorn; unknown letters, 16th Connecticut Regimental File, Antietam National Battlefield; Nettles, letter.
266. Unknown letter, 16th Connecticut Regimental File, Antietam National Battlefield; Bauer, letter to Bauer.
267. *Final Attack Trail*, 6.
268. Gordon, *Broken Regiment*, 37.
269. Bingman, letter to father; Gordon, *Broken Regiment*, 39.
270. Priest, *16th Connecticut Volunteer Infantry*, September 26 diary entry.
271. Belden, Diary; Cuzner, letter to Van Dorn.
272. Robbins, letter to sister; Gordon, *Broken Regiment*, 41.
273. Gordon, *Broken Regiment*, 34, 257; Croffut and Morris, *Military and Cultural History*, 271.
274. Cuzner, letter to Van Dorn.
275. Allen, *Forty-Six Months*, 143; Kolakowski, "Success and Failure," 27.
276. Spooner, "Maryland Campaign," 232.
277. Gordon, *Broken Regiment*, 36.
278. Allen, *Forty-Six Months*, 143.
279. Allen, *Forty-Six Months*, 144; O.R. 19, part 1, 456.
280. Allen, *Forty-Six Months*, 144–45.
281. Spooner, "Maryland Campaign," 231.
282. Carman, *Maryland Campaign*, 466–67.
283. Pawlak, "Forty-Acre Cornfield," 18–21; O'Reilly, email to author, March 10, 2021.
284. Keely, Civil War Diary; Wardlow, Diary.
285. Mockbee, *Historical Sketch*.
286. Pawlak, "Desperation," 19–22, 27–31.
287. Spooner, "Maryland Campaign," 232–33, 235.
288. Caldwell, *Brigade of South Carolinians*, 77–78.
289. Caldwell, *Brigade of South Carolinians*, 79, 29; Baracz, "Beyond Burnside's Bridge."

290. *Voices of the Civil War*, 130–31.
291. *Recollections and Reminiscences*, 3:482.
292. Cox, *Reminiscences*, 656; Walcott, *21st Regiment Massachusetts Volunteers*, 203.

Chapter 7

293. *Interpretive Plan, Antietam National Battlefield.*
294. Almon, letter to parents; Brunson, *Pee Dee Light Artillery*, 21.
295. Unknown letter, Sixteenth Connecticut, Sixteenth Connecticut Regimental File, Antietam National Battlefield.
296. Compton, *Autobiography*, 105.
297. Longacre, *Antietam to Fort Fisher*, 38–39.
298. Johnston, *Confederate Boy*, 146; Priest, *George Wren's Diary*, 75.
299. Liska and Perlotto, *Eighth Connecticut Volunteer Infantry*, 85; Marsh, letter to Marsh.
300. *Excursion and Reunion*, 21; Croffut and Morris, *Military and Cultural History*, 275.
301. Burnham, letter to his mother; Kellogg, Diary.
302. Blakeslee, *Sixteenth Connecticut Volunteers,* Pomeroy, letter to Aldrich.
303. Burnham, letter to his mother; Blakeslee, *Sixteenth Connecticut Volunteers*, 21.
304. Elliot, Burial Map.
305. Lord, *Ninth New Hampshire Volunteers*, 112.
306. O.R. 19, part 1, 888; Murfin, *Gleam of Bayonets*, appendix D, 374.
307. Caldwell, *Brigade of South Carolinians*, 78; O.R. 19, part 1, 989.
308. Carman, *Maryland Campaign*, 436; Johnston, "Battle of Antietam," 28; Hunter, "High Private's Sketch," 18; Fogle, letter to Fogle; O.R. supplement, 51, 162–63.
309. Gordon, *Broken Regiment*, 35; Williams, "Rodman's Brigade"; Croffut and Morris, *Military and Cultural History*, 276; Priest, *Antietam*, 341; Schildt, *Antietam Through the Years*, 32.
310. Graham, *Ninth Regiment*, 327; Priest, *Antietam*, 340.
311. Priest, *Antietam*, 341; Walton, "30th Ohio."
312. *Thirty-Fifth Massachusetts*, 53; Parker, *51st Regiment of Pennsylvania Volunteers*, 236; Priest, *Antietam*, 340.
313. Cowie, *Hell Came to Sharpsburg*, 75, 241–42.
314. K.M. Walker, *Antietam Farmsteads*, 103; Cowie, *Hell Came to Sharpsburg*, 127, 244, 267.

315. At Fredericksburg, the Ninth Corps assaulted Marye's Heights, yet the story of this attack is not nearly as studied or celebrated as the attacks of the Second and Fifth Corps.
316. O.R. 19, part 1, 718; O'Reilly, email to author.
317. Gordon, *Broken Regiment*, 37–38, 61; *Excursion and Reunion*, 19–20.
318. Gavin, *Campaigning with the Roundheads*, 167.
319. Schildt, *Antietam Through the Years*, 80, 82.
320. Schildt, *Antietam Through the Years*, 26; *Souvenir of Excursion*, 5; Banks, "Antietam Monument Photo." It is interesting to note that the veterans believed the land where they fought would never be preserved, with access to all the ground, and instead were willing to put up their monuments on ground far from where they fought.
321. Snell and Brown, *Antietam National Battlefield*, 175.
322. Schildt, *Antietam Through the Years*, 30; *Souvenir of Excursion*, 10.
323. *Souvenir of Excursion*, 48–49.
324. Schildt, *Monuments at Antietam*, 97; Cunningham and Miller, *Antietam*, 21.
325. Adams, *Monuments at Antietam*, 63.
326. Jones, "Address," 532.
327. Johnston, "Battle of Antietam," 28.
328. Hunter, "High Private's Sketch," 16.
329. Motlow, "Campaigns in Northern Virginia," 310; Mockbee, "Sharpsburg," 160.
330. Richardson, "Gen. A.P. Hill at Sharpsburg," 346.
331. Horton and Teverbaugh, *Eleventh Regiment Ohio Volunteer Infantry*, 75–76; Brinkerhoff, *Thirtieth Regiment Ohio Volunteer Infantry*, 46.
332. Benning, "Notes," 393.
333. Napier, "McIntosh's Battery," 429; Jones and Evans, *Treasured Reminiscences*, 43–44.
334. Johnston, "Battle of Antietam," 28; McIntosh, "McIntosh's Battery," 204.
335. *Souvenir of Excursion*, 25–26.
336. Schildt, *Monuments*, 32.
337. "Our Army Correspondence," *Columbia Spy*.
338. Hartwig, *I Dread the Thought*, 531.
339. *General Management Plan*, 11.
340. *Interpretive Plan, Antietam National Battlefield*, 47, 39.
341. *Interpretive Plan, Antietam National Battlefield*, 63; *Visitor Access*, 9, 22–23.

BIBLIOGRAPHY

Primary Sources

Albert, Allen D. *History of the Forty-Fifth Regiment of Pennsylvania Veteran Volunteer Infantry.* Grit Publishing, 1912.

Allen, George H. *Forty-Six Months with the Fourth Rhode Island Volunteers in the War of 1861 to '65.* J.A. and R.A. Reed, 1887.

Almon, Reed. Reed Almon to parents, September 21, 1862. Eighty-Ninth New York Regimental File, Antietam National Battlefield.

Arnold, Jennie P. "At Antietam." *National Tribune* (Washington, D.C.), October 18, 1888.

Banks, John. "View Digitally Restored Antietam Monument Photo from 1894." *John Banks' Civil War Blog*, February 11, 2018. https://john-banks.blogspot.com.

Bauer, Jacob. Jacob Bauer to Sarah Bauer, September 18, 1862. Sixteenth Connecticut Regimental File, Antietam National Battlefield.

Belden, Elizur. Diary. Vol. I. Elizur Belden diaries, 1862–1864, Ms 41878, Connecticut Museum of Culture and History.

Bennett, Edwin. Edwin Bennett to Titus Bennett, September 28, 1862. Fifty-First Pennsylvania Regimental File, Antietam National Battlefield.

Benning, H.L. "Notes by General H.L. Benning on the Battle of Sharpsburg." *Southern Historical Society Papers* 16 (1888): 393–95.

Bingham, Wells. Wells Bingham to Father, September 20, 1862. Connecticut Historical Society.

Blakeslee, B.F. *History of the Sixteenth Connecticut Volunteers.* Case, Lockwood & Brainard, 1875.

———. "The Sixteenth at Antietam." *Hartford (CT) Daily Times*, February 13, 1871.

Bolton, William. War Diary. Fifty-First Pennsylvania Regimental File, Antietam National Battlefield.

Bosbyshell, Oliver. *The 48th in the War.* Avil, 1895.

Brinkerhoff, Henry B. *History of the Thirtieth Regiment Ohio Volunteer Infantry.* James W. Osgood, 1863.

Brock, R.A. "The Battle of Antietam." *Southern Historical Society Papers* 31 (1903): 37–43.

Brock, R.A., ed. "Lieutenant General A.P. Hill." *Southern Historical Society Papers* 19 (January 1891): 178–86.

Brunson, Joseph W. *Pee Dee Light Artillery of Maxcey Gregg's (Late Samuel McGowan's) Brigade.* Confederate Regimental Series No. 4. Morningside House, 1983.

"The Burke Sharpshooters." *Confederate Veteran* 32 (1924): 464.

Burnham, John. John Burnham to mother and family. October 4, 1862. George Whitney Civil War Collection, Connecticut State Library.

Carman, Ezra A. *The Maryland Campaign.* Vol. 2. Savas Beatic, 2012.

"The Colors of the Ninth Regiment, New York Zouaves." Ninth New York Regimental File, Antietam National Battlefield.

Columbia (PA) Spy. "Our Army Correspondence." October 11, 1862.

Compton, Samuel. *Autobiography.* Samuel Compton Papers, Manuscript Department, Rubenstein Library, Duke University.

Cox, Jacob D. "The Battle of Antietam." In *Battles and Leaders of the Civil War*. Vol. 2. Century Company, 1887.

———. *Military Reminiscences of the Civil War.* Vol. 1. Scribner's Sons, 1900.

Croffut, W.A., and John M. Morris. *The Military and Cultural History of Connecticut During the War of 1861–1865.* Ledyard Bill, 1868.

Cunningham, David, and Wells W. Miller. *Antietam.* Report of the Ohio Antietam Battlefield Commission. Springfield, 1904.

Cuzner, John B. John B. Cuzner to Ellen Van Dorn, September 22, 1862. Cuzner Letters and Papers, Connecticut Historical Society.

Daly, Louise Haskell. *Alexander Cheves Haskell: The Portrait of a Man.* Broadfoot, 1989.

Dimon, Theodore. "A Federal Surgeon at Sharpsburg." Edited by James I. Robertson Jr. *Civil War History* 6, no. 2 (June 1960): 134–46.

Dugan, Ivy. Ivy Dugan to the *Central Georgian*. October 14, 1862. University of Georgia Library.

Durkin, Joseph T., ed. *John Dooley: Confederate Soldier.* Georgetown University Press, 1945.

Elliot, S.T. Burial Map. New York Public Library.

Evans, Clement, ed. *Confederate Military History.* Vol. 5. Broadfoot, 1987.

Excursion and Reunion, Antietam Battlefield. Case, Lockwood and Brainard, 1889.

"The Fiftieth Georgia Regiment in Maryland and Virginia." Undated newspaper article, Fiftieth Georgia Regimental File, Antietam National Battlefield.

Fogle, Theodore. Theodore Fogle to Dr. J. Fogle. September 28, 1862. Emory University Archives.

Gould, Joseph. *The Story of the 48th*. Regimental Association, 1908.

Graham, Matthew J. Matthew J. Graham to Rush C. Hawkins. September 27, 1894. Brown University Library.

———. *The Ninth Regiment, New York Volunteers.* M. Graham, 1900.

Hine, Burton. Diary. Eighty-Ninth New York Regimental File, Antietam National Battlefield.

History of the Thirty-Fifth Massachusetts Volunteers. Mill, Knight, 1884.

Horton, J.H., and Solomon Teverbaugh. *A History of the Eleventh Regiment Ohio Volunteer Infantry.* W.J. Shuey, 1866.

Hudson, John W. John W. Hudson to Sophy Hudson. October 16, 1862. Vertical File Collection, Western Maryland Room, Antietam Battlefield Filing Cabinet, File ABC, WMR-1-12, Washington County Library, Hagerstown, Maryland.

Hunter, Alexander. "A High Private's Sketch of Sharpsburg." *Southern Historical Society Papers* 11 (1883): 10–21.

Jackman, Lyman. *History of the Sixth New Hampshire Regiment.* Republican Press, 1891.

Johnston, David E. "Concerning the Battle of Sharpsburg." *Confederate Veteran* 6, no. 1 (January 1898): 27–29.

———. *The Story of a Confederate Boy in the Civil War.* Glass & Prudhomme, 1914.

Jones, William, ed. "Address of General B.T. Johnson." *Southern Historical Society Papers* 12 (January–December 1884): 500–36.

Jones, W.E., and C.D. Evans, eds. *Treasured Reminiscences.* State Co., 1911.

Keely, John. Civil War Diary. Bound Volume 127, Fredericksburg Spotsylvania National Military Park.

Kellogg, Robert. Diary, September 1862. Robert Hale Kellogg papers, 1862–1931. Box 1, Folder 1, Ms 68013, Connecticut Museum of Culture and History.

Lokey, J.W. *My Experiences in the War Between the States.* Self-published, 1959.

Lord, Edward O., ed. *History of the Ninth New Hampshire Volunteers in the War of the Rebellion.* Wakefield, Willcox and Blaisdell, 1895.

Marsh, Wolcott P. Wolcott P. Marsh to Anna Marsh, September 22, 1862. Eighth Connecticut Regimental File, Antietam National Battlefield.

McIntosh, D.G. "McIntosh's Battery at Sharpsburg." *Confederate Veteran* 20, no. 5 (May 1912): 204.

McRae, George. "Benning's Brigade in the Wilderness." Undated newspaper article, Twentieth Georgia Regimental File, Antietam National Battlefield.

Merriman, George. George Merriman to Mary Merriman, September 24, 1862. Connecticut Historical Society.

Mixson, Frank. *Reminiscences of a Private.* State Company, 1910.

Mockbee, Robert T. *Historical Sketch of the 14th Tennessee Regiment of Infantry, C.S.A., 1861–1865.* Fourteenth Tennessee Regimental File, Antietam National Battlefield.

———. "Why Sharpsburg Was 'A Drawn Battle.'" *Confederate Veteran* 16, no. 4 (April 1908): 160.

Motlow, Felix. "Campaigns in Northern Virginia." *Confederate Veteran* 2, no. 10 (October 1894): 310–12.

Napier, J.L. "McIntosh's Battery at Sharpsburg." *Confederate Veteran* 19, no. 9 (September 1911): 429.

National Defender (Philadelphia, PA). "Letter from 51st Penna." October 14, 1862.

National Tribune. "Fighting Them Over." April 25, 1889.

Nettleton, Samuel Jay. Letter to brother and friends, September 24, 1862. Connecticut Historical Society.

New York State Military Museum and Veterans Research Center. "9th New York Infantry Regiment's Civil War Historical Sketch." https://museum.dmna.ny.gov/unit-history/infantry/9th-infantry-regiment/historical-sketch.

Overton, Edward. Letter to U.S. Department of War. June 21, 1893. Fiftieth Pennsylvania Regimental File, Antietam National Battlefield.

Parker, Thomas. *History of the 51st Regiment of Pennsylvania Volunteers and Veteran Volunteers.* King and Baird, 1869.

Pendleton, William T. Letter to unknown recipient, September 22, 1862. William T. Pendleton Papers, University of North Carolina Wilson Special Collection Library.

Pomeroy, Julian. Julian Pomeroy to Sarah Aldrich, September 29, 1862. Connecticut Historical Society.

Porter, Thomas. *History of the Fifty-First Regiment of Pennsylvania Volunteers.* King and Baird, 1869.

Priest, John M., ed. *George Wren's Diary.* White Mane Press, 1990.

Richardson, C.A. "General A.P. Hill at Sharpsburg." *Confederate Veteran* 16, no. 7 (July 1908): 346.

———. "Incidents at Sharpsburg." *Confederate Veteran* 15, no. 8 (August 1907): 380.

Robbins, George. George Robbins to sister, September 23, 1862. George Robbins papers, 1861–1865, Ms 84647, Connecticut Museum of Culture and History.

Savannah (GA) Republican. "The Fiftieth Georgia Regiment in Virginia and Maryland." October 16, 1862.

Schmitt, Martin F., ed. *General George Crook, His Autobiography.* University of Oklahoma Press, 1946.

Souvenir of Excursion to Antietam and Dedication of Monuments of the 8th, 11th, 14th, and 16th Regiments of Connecticut Volunteers. Souvenir booklet, 1894.

Spooner, Henry. "The Maryland Campaign with the Fourth Rhode Island." In *Personal Narratives of Events of the War of the Rebellion, Being Papers Read Before the Rhode Island Soldiers and Sailors Historical Society*. Vol. 9. Snow & Farnham, 1903.

Thomas David. Letter Elias Daniel, October 1862. Ninth New York Regimental File, Antietam National Battlefield.

Thompson, David L. "With Burnside at Antietam." In *Battles and Leaders of the Civil War*. Vol. 2. Century Company, 1887.

Tillinghart, G.F. "Fighting Them Over." *National Tribune* (Washington, D.C.), December 30, 1886.

Todd, William. *The Seventy-Ninth New York Volunteers in the War of Rebellion.* Brandon & Barton, 1886.

Unidentified newspaper article. Fiftieth Pennsylvania Regimental File, Antietam National Battlefield.

Unknown letters. "The cannonading at this time was most terrible…" Sixteenth Connecticut Regimental File, Antietam National Battlefield.

Unknown letter. "A great battle all around me…" Ninth New York Regimental File, Antietam National Battlefield.

Voices of the Civil War: Antietam. Time-Life Books, 1996.

Walcott, Charles F. *History of the 21st Regiment Massachusetts Volunteers.* Houghton Mifflin, 1882.

Walker, John G. "Sharpsburg." In *Battles and Leaders of the Civil War*. Vol. 2. Century Company, 1887.

Walton, J.K. "The 30th Ohio." *National Tribune* (Washington, D.C.), December 31, 1885.

War of the Rebellion: The Official Records of the Union and Confederate Armies. Series 1, Vol. 19, Parts 1 and 2. Government Printing Office, 1887.

War of the Rebellion: The Official Records of the Union and Confederate Armies. Supplement, Vol. 51, Part 1, Vol. 3. Government Printing Office, 1887.

Wardlow, Andrew. Diary. Fourteenth South Carolina Regimental File, Antietam National Battlefield.

Watts. Watts to *Plain Dealer* (Cleveland, OH), September 30, 1862.

Whisterer, Frederick, ed. *New York in the War of the Rebellion.* J.B. Lyon, 1912.

Whitney, J.H.E. *The Hawkins Zouaves.* Self-published, 1866.

Williams, Horace N. "Rodman's Brigade at Antietam." *National Tribune* (Washington, D.C.), December 9, 1886.

Secondary Sources

Adams, Charles S., ed. *The Monuments at Antietam: Sharpsburg's Silent Sentinels.* Self-published, 2000.

Armstrong, William H. *Major McKinley*. Kent State University Press, 2000.

Baldwin, James, III. *The Struck Eagle*. Burd Street Press, 1996.

Baracz, Brian. "Beyond Burnside's Bridge." HistoryNet, September 17, 2018. https://www.historynet.com/beyond-burnside-bridge.

Bell, Robert T. *11th Virginia Infantry*. H.E. Howard, 1985.

Caldwell, J.F.J. *History of a Brigade of South Carolinians*. Morningside, 1984.

Cavanaugh, Michael A., and William Marvel. *The Petersburg Campaign: The Battle of the Crater*. H.E. Howard, 1989.

Clark, Walter, ed. *Histories of the Several Regiments and Battalions from North Carolina in the Great War.* Vols. 1 and 2. E.M. Uzzell, 1901.

Clary, James B. *A History of the 15th South Carolina Infantry*. South Carolina Department of Archives and History, 2007.

Clemmens, Thomas. Email to author. May 14, 2009.

Cowie, Steven. *When Hell Came to Sharpsburg*. Savas Beatie, 2024.

Dameron, Dave. *Benning's Brigade*. Vol. 1. Reprint Company, 1997.

The Final Attack Trail. Western Maryland Interpretive Association, n.d.

Frassanitto, William A. *Antietam*. Charles Scribner's Sons, 1988.

Gavin, William Gilfillan. *Campaigning with the Roundheads*. Morningside, 1989.

General Management Plan/Final Environmental Impact Statement, Antietam National Battlefield. National Park Service, 1992.

Gordon, Leslie. *A Broken Regiment*. Louisiana State University Press, 2014.

Gottfried, Braley M. *The Maps of Antietam*. Savas Beatie, 2012.

Greene, A. Wilson. "I Fought the Battle Splendidly." In *Antietam*, edited by Gary W. Gallagher. Kent State University Press, 1989.

———. *Infantryman Pettit*. White Mane, 1990.

Hardy, Michael C. *General Lee's Immortals*. Savas Beatie, 2018.

———. *The Thirty-Seventh North Carolina Troops*. McFarland, 2009.

Hartwig, Scott D. *I Dread the Thought of the Place*. Johns Hopkins University Press, 2023.

———. *To Antietam Creek*. Johns Hopkins University Press, 2012.

Interpretive Plan, Antietam National Battlefield. National Park Service, 1996.

Johnson, Charles F. *The Long Roll*. Carabelle Books, 1986.

Johnson, Curt, and Richard C. Anderson Jr. *Artillery Hell*. Texas A&M University, 1995.

Jordan, Weymouth, ed. *North Carolina Troops, 1861–1865: A Roster*. Vol. 6. North Carolina Office of Archives and History, 1990.

Kolakowski, Christopher L. "Success and Failure: The Ninth Corps in Maryland, 1862." Paper for Emory and Henry College, 1998.

Liska, William A., and Kim L. Perlotto. *The Eighth Connecticut Volunteer Infantry in the Civil War*. McFarland, 2023.

Longacre, Edward, ed. *From Antietam to Fort Fisher*. Associate University Press, 1985.

Marvel, William. *Burnside*. University of North Carolina Press, 1991.

———. *Race of the Soil*. Broadfoot Publishing, 1988.

Murfin, James V. *The Gleam of Bayonets*. Louisiana State University Press, 1965.

O'Reilly, Frank. Email to author. March 10, 2021.

Pawlak, Kevin. "A Bridge for Whiskey: The 51st Pennsylvania and Its Famous Request Examined." *Emerging Civil War* (blog), January 28, 2021. https://emergingcivilwar.com.

———. "Deception in the Forty-Acre Cornfield?" *Antietam Journal* 3 (September 2022): 18–33.

———. Emails to author. February 21, 2022, and June 22, 2024.

Pawlak, Kevin, and Dan Welch. *Ohio at Antietam*. The History Press, 2021.

Priest, John M. *Antietam: The Soldiers' Battle*. Oxford University Press, 1989.

Priest, John M., ed. *16th Connecticut Volunteer Infantry: Sergeant William H. Relyea*. Burd Street Press, 2002.

Recollections and Reminiscences. Vol. 3. South Carolina Division, United Daughters of the Confederacy, 1992.

Recollections and Reminiscences. Vol. 5. South Carolina Division, United Daughters of the Confederacy, 1994.

Riggs, David F. *7th Virginia Infantry*. H.E. Howard, 1982.

Rosebrock, James. "A.P. Hill or Artillery: Stopping the Ninth Corps at Antietam." Antietam Institute Fall Conference, Shepherd University, Shepherdstown, West Virginia, September 28, 2024.

Schildt, John W. *Antietam Through the Years*. N.p., 2008.

———. *Monuments at Antietam*. Antietam Publications, 1991.

———. *The Ninth Corps at Antietam*. Antietam Publications, 1988.

Sears, Stephen W. *Landscape Turned Red*. Ticknor & Fields, 1983.

Snell, Charles W., and Sharon A. Brown. *Antietam National Battlefield and National Cemetery, an Administrative History*. National Park Service, 1986.

Toney, Keith. "Dying as Brave Men Should Die." *Journal of the American Civil War: The Maryland Campaign of 1862 and Its Aftermath* 6, no. 2: 89–188.

Troiani, Don. *Soldiers in America*. Stackpole, 1998.

Tucker, Phillip Thomas. *Burnside's Bridge*. Stackpolc, 2011.

Union Advance Trail. Western Maryland Interpretive Association, n.d.

Virtual Antietam Blog. "Antietam Monuments in Connecticut Park." May 3, 2024. https://www.virtualantietam.com.

Visitor Access and Circulation Plan. National Park Service, 2018.

Walker, Kevin M. *A Guide to the Battlefield Landscape: Antietam Farmsteads*. Western Maryland Interpretive Association, 2010.

Wallace, Lee A., Jr. *1st Virginia Infantry*. H.E. Howard, 1985.

———. *17th Virginia Infantry*. H.E. Howard, 1990.

White, Ralph G. *24th Virginia Infantry*. H.E. Howard, 1987.

INDEX

A

B

C

D

E

F

G

H

J

K

L

M

P

R

S

T

W

ABOUT THE AUTHOR

Robert M. Dunkerly is a historian who is active in historic preservation. He has a degree in history from St. Vincent Collee and a master's in historic preservation from Middle Tennessee State University. In his career, he was worked at a dozen historic sites conducting research, archaeology and interpretation. He has authored seventeen books about the American Revolution, the Civil War and other topics. Dunkerly has served as president of the Richmond Civil War Round Table and taught classes at the Virginia Museum of History and Culture and Central Virginia Community College, and he writes for the *Emerging Civil War* and *Revolutionary War* blogs. He has visited over one thousand battlefields worldwide and enjoys visiting battlefields, bookstores and breweries—not necessarily in that order.